Grammar Survival

A Teacher's Toolkit

Grammar Survival

A Teacher's Toolkit

Geoff Barton

David Fulton Publishers

David Fulton Publishers Ltd
The Chiswick Centre, 414 Chiswick High Road, London W4 5TF

www.fultonpublishers.co.uk

David Fulton Publishers is a division of Granada Learning Limited, part of ITV plc.

British Library Cataloguing in Publication Data
A catalogue record for this book is available from the British Library.

ISBN: 1 84312 343 6

10 9 8 7 6 5 4 3 2 1

Typeset by FiSH Books, Enfield, Middlesex
Printed and bound in Great Britain

Contents

WRITING

READING

Introduction

Many of us were taught almost nothing formally about English grammar. What knowledge we have we frequently acquired from lessons in French or German. As a result, there is a generation of pupils, and now teachers, who feel de-skilled and insecure when it comes to understanding how our language works.

So this book is for you (and for me), self-taught in aspects of grammar, and lamenting the fact that for too long we have been too cautious in using grammar in our teaching.

It is important, before we get started, to state a few basic principles:

- Knowing about grammar is important for teachers and pupils, but it isn't an end in itself. This book is selective: I've only chosen those bits of grammar that I think will make a difference to your pupils' reading and writing.

- Grammar shouldn't dominate your teaching: all the other stuff – talking about literature, listening to pupils, reading great texts, watching worthwhile films, exploring language, having fun – these are at the core of our work as English teachers. Grammar can enhance all of this, but it doesn't replace it.

- This book is all about impact: don't teach any grammar for the sake of it (or to impress your headteacher or parents). Teach what will help your pupils to be better communicators and ignore the rest.

- Remember the importance of cross-curricular links. The compartmentalisation of English and other subjects does us few favours. Help your pupils to make connections across subjects by focusing on the reading and writing skills they will need for, say, reading a historical document or writing a technology evaluation.

Grammar Survival is closely aligned to the Framework for Teaching English. It aims to help you translate that document into a template for lively, informative and productive lessons. Again, I've chosen the bits of the Framework that I think need most explanation and certainly will have a most positive effect in class.

Every section has an introduction and concludes with a summary. Each two-page spread has a theory page (what you need to know) and a practice page (how to apply the knowledge in class). There is also a glossary and list of recommended reading.

When I started, I tried to write a serious book about grammar. It was too dull and too formal. I soon gave up and wrote the kind of book I wished was available when I trained to teach English, some 20 years ago. I hope it works for you.

Geoff Barton
Suffolk
April 2005

Foreword

Like many teachers, my first lesson in grammar took place when I was teaching. Until the various literacy strategies of recent years, the formal teaching of grammar was a hit-and-miss affair. It was lost in the sterile debate, in which the rejection of formal grammar seemed linked to notions of formality with a starched collar and a stick up it, somewhere. Surveying the scene in 1998, the QCA found a lack of confidence in this area, noting teachers lacked confidence where 'sentence structure had not formed part of their own education'. That was me! I came to the subject late and have since trained myself up to teach it and train others to teach on it. At times like this you need a good, brief and readable guide. This new one from Geoff Barton does just that. It also moves us beyond debating whether subject knowledge stifles creativity or deadens our experience of language. The examples are contemporary, as when paragraphing is demonstrated through discussing reality TV. The skills presented home in on the crafting of language, and throughout the book he is asking us to apply the material by cutting up texts, exploring dialects through literature and teaching punctuation through scary story openings.

This practical guide smacks of the work of someone who can't get too theoretical because next Monday he'll be joining the rest of us in a real school teaching real kids. I know Geoff would thoroughly endorse the words of Maya Angelou, who once described the wordcraft of a writer in terms of grammar leading to revolution: 'I know that I must select studiously the nouns, pronouns, verbs, adverbs, etcetera, and by a careful syntactical arrangement make readers laugh, reflect or riot.' Choose which of those you will resort to, but enjoy this book and let it bring language to life.

Huw Thomas
St John's Primary School, Sheffield
April 2005

Sentence Level Grammar

INTRODUCTION

This is the area of grammar that people often worry most about ... which is why I have put it first.

This section takes the sentence level section of the Framework for Teaching English and provides guidance on making it work in class. Remember the importance of the teaching sequence. Working on grammar isn't like lobbing a smoke-bomb into the room, then standing back to see the effect. It needs active and frequent teacher guidance and is strongly underpinned by the approach of the Secondary Strategy.

In practice this means that you should aim for:

- More explicit teaching, with attention to word and sentence level skills
- An emphasis on learning rather than just completing coursework or getting through set texts
- Use of the whole lesson for planned teaching, and less time spent on unplanned circulation around the groups, making optimum use of the teacher's expertise and time
- Increased opportunities for whole class interaction
- Frequent, fast-paced revision of insecure skills at word and sentence level
- The use of shared time rather than independent time to ensure the transfer of skills into everyday use

So, give plenty of emphasis to:

- Shared reading and writing – in which the teacher demonstrates and models the process of comprehension or composition with the whole class
- Guided reading and writing – in which the teacher dedicates substantial time in the lesson to stretch and support a particular group
- Plenaries to consolidate the learning objectives
- Investigations – in which pupils explore language and work out its rules and conventions
- Whole class interaction – in which all pupils are expected to respond, rather than individuals
- Specific achievable targets – for groups and sometimes for individual pupils

These principles of the Secondary Strategy underpin the approach to grammar throughout the whole of this book.

TEACHING ABOUT SENTENCES

Defining what a sentence is is not as simple as you would think. In fact, it can prove surprisingly difficult to pin down.

However, if pupils are to have success in their writing across any subjects, they will need a good working understanding of what sentences are and how they can be used imaginatively.

Three key ingredients of sentences:

- A sentence makes sense. It is grammatical.
- It can stand alone.
- It contains a verb or verb chain.

<table>
<tr>
<td align="center"></td>
<td align="center"></td>
</tr>
<tr>
<td align="center">The fly buzzed around my ear.
I walked into the room.
I walked.</td>
<td align="center">Around buzzed the fly my ear.
I walked into.
Walked.</td>
</tr>
</table>

The use of the term 'verb chain' is useful. It refers to the collection of words built around the verb to show tense. Here are different verb chains:

- I have walked into the room.
- I am walking into the room.
- I was walking into the room.
- I used to walk into the room.

Of course, writers will sometimes use verbless sentences deliberately in texts to create an impact:

> **The night fell. <u>Hideously quickly</u>.**

Verbless sentences are also common in signs, greetings and advertising:

- No smoking
- Hello
- The ultimate driving machine

You will need to know about:

- Simple, compound and complex sentences
- The importance of sentence variety

The next spreads will help to build your knowledge.

TEACHING ABOUT SENTENCES

BEFORE THE LESSON

It's important not to see sentences as a one-off 'quick hit'. A single lesson will not, in itself, help pupils to use sentences consistently. Therefore plan to teach, re-teach and reinforce the knowledge, through starter activities, reminders when setting up written assignments, and in your marking.

STARTERS

Sometimes a reassuring approach to grammar is to use 'bad' rather than 'good' models. They can reassure pupils. So get them to think up nonsense sentences – sentences which cannot be classified as sentences because they simply do not make sense, like this:

- On station man I saw the a
- Mum my home at TV sat watching
- The at back house of the

Make it a game, where pupils in small groups untangle the nonsense sentences to decide whether they can make each nonsense sentence into a real sentence. Get them holding up a green card (or any green object, such as a pencil case or book)) if they can, and a red card (or item) if they cannot. Make it a game. Flash each nonsense sentence on to an OHP or whiteboard. Give pupils 10 seconds to decide whether it makes sense or not.

The next stage is to encourage pupils to describe why a sentence does not make sense, so you could give them labels:

A: This doesn't make sense at all.

B: This is a phrase, not a sentence.

C: This isn't a sentence because it doesn't contain a verb chain (a minor sentence).

Get them categorising their responses like this, sharpening their ability to recognise sentences, minor sentences (no verb chain) and non-sentences.

RESEARCH

Focus on the way advertising slogans use sentences. Encourage pupils to collect as many examples as possible and then, again, to categorise them as sentences or minor sentences. You can find lots of examples by using a search engine and typing in 'famous advertising slogans'.

THEORY

TEACHING ABOUT CLAUSES

We can't really understand sentences without knowing about clauses. This is a part of grammar which sometimes scares people, especially terms like 'subordinate clauses', but in fact it's straightforward.

Clauses are the building-blocks of sentences. They always contain a verb. Sometimes clauses can stand alone (finite clauses) and sometimes they only make sense as part of a larger sentence (non-finite clauses). Some examples:

Finite clauses (can stand on their own and make sense)	Non-finite clauses (only make sense as part of a larger sentence)
She eats salad.	Eating her salad
He cried softly.	Crying softly
He was obsessed by her.	Obsessed by her

There are two types of clause: coordinated and subordinate.

Coordinated clauses link ideas together, giving them equal status. They use coordinating conjunctions like 'and', 'but' or 'or':

> **I like fish and I like cheese.**

You can see these are equal status, with neither idea being more important than the other. You could write it as: 'I like cheese and I like fish'.

SUBORDINATE CLAUSES

These clauses give us background information to the main clause. In these examples the subordinate clause is italicised:

> **I like cheese *although I eat too much of it.***

> ***Because I like cheese*, I eat lots of it.**

> ***After eating too much cheese*, I felt ill.**

You need to know about clauses because they will help you to teach pupils how to create sentence variety.

TEACHING ABOUT CLAUSES

BEFORE THE LESSON

Be clear in your own mind what the objective is. Pupils need to know about clauses as a building-block of sentences. The aim is to improve their own writing, not simply to be able to spot types of clauses. Most useful would be for them to distinguish between coordinated clauses (joined by 'and', 'but' and 'or') and subordinate clauses. It is subordinate clauses that will give most depth and variety to their writing.

READING

You might ask pupils to look at two contrasting texts, one written entirely as simple sentences, the other as a long sequence of coordinated clauses. Which do they prefer? Why? What is the effect of each style? What would they think of a text which was written mostly in this style?

Simple sentences	Coordinated clauses in compound sentences
I went to the zoo. I saw lots of animals. Some were big. Some were small. Some were smelly. I had an ice cream. I fell over. I came home.	I went to the zoo and I saw lots of animals and some were big and some were small and some were smelly. I had an ice cream and I fell over and I came home.

Set pupils the challenge of making the two texts more interesting by using some subordinating connectives:

because	unless
until	after
when	if
although	while
where	in order to
since	rather than
as	

Remind pupils that that some of these connectives may work at the start of sentences as well as in the middle.

Remember that at this stage we want pupils to explore the effect and to build their own language confidence, so respond positively to new sentences.

THEORY

TEACHING ABOUT SENTENCE TYPES

WHAT YOU NEED TO KNOW:

Sentences are made up of clauses, which are units of words that are smaller than sentences built around verbs or verb chains.

*   Simple sentences contain just one clause.

*   Compound sentences consist of two or more main clauses loosely joined by coordinating conjunctions – 'and', 'but', 'or'.

*   Complex sentences consist of two or more clauses – a main clause (which carries the main meaning of the sentence) and subordinate clauses (which carry the background information).

All of these are explained more fully in this and the next few spreads.

TEACHING ABOUT SENTENCE TYPES

BEFORE THE LESSON

Don't see this topic as a 'quick hit'. Plan a sequence of activities which allow pupils to explore sentence types in depth. Lively and varied teaching and learning approaches are essential, so aim to use:

- Direction: to ensure pupils know what they are doing, and why
- Demonstration: to show pupils how effective readers and writers work
- Modelling: to explain the rules and conventions of language and texts
- Scaffolding: to support pupils' early efforts and build security and confidence
- Explanation: to clarify and exemplify the best ways of working
- Questioning: to probe, draw out or extend pupils' thinking
- Exploration: to encourage critical thinking and generalisation
- Investigation: to encourage enquiry and self-help
- Discussion: to shape and challenge developing ideas
- Reflection and evaluation: to help pupils to learn from experience, successes and mistakes

In practice this might mean:

- Using a sequence of starter activities in which pupils explore, rewrite or categorise different types of sentences.
- They could separate simple from complex sentences.
- They might respond to a test written entirely in simple sentences, with one group rewriting it in compound sentences (clauses joined by 'and', 'but' and 'or'); another looking at rewriting it with complex sentences.
- They could gather examples of signs and slogans, deciding which are sentences and which are minor sentences (no verbs).
- They might compare texts written for different audiences or ages – for example a story for a three-year old versus a story for a 13-year-old, comparing the sentence types in the opening paragraphs.

Starter activities are an ideal way to keep re-visiting the topic, building confidence, investigating different aspects of the subject, and really embedding different structures in your pupils' minds.

Also, keep relating sentence types to their context – to the decisions writers make according to their purpose and audience. Compare sentence types in different newspapers; produce charts of your findings; take a genuinely exploratory approach in order to build pupils' confidence and familiarity with the subject.

THEORY

TEACHING ABOUT SIMPLE SENTENCES

A simple sentence has a **subject** and a **verb** (or verb chain). There may be other elements in the sentence but as long as there is only one verb or verb chain it is a **simple sentence**.

> The dog <u>barked</u>.
> The baby <u>woke up</u>.
> The dog <u>whined</u>.

Simple sentences are important for adding sentence variety. It is a striking fact that grade A* writers use more simple sentences than those writing at grade C – so we need to encourage our pupils to use them judiciously, aware of the impact they can make.

There are two main areas of knowledge you need:

(a)   How simple sentences can be expanded in a number of ways:

You can change the verb chain, like this:

The dog <u>barked</u>.

The dog <u>was barking</u>.

The dog <u>has barked</u>.

The dog <u>was going to bark</u>.

You can add adjectives before the noun, adverbs around the verb, and a prepositional phrase:

The dog <u>barked</u>.

becomes . . .

The <u>old</u> dog <u>barked loudly in the street</u>.

(b)   The stylistic effects of simple sentences:

They add clarity and precision. They can simplify complicated texts, especially if used at the beginning and end of sentences. They can build suspense in stories.

However, they can also become repetitive and monotonous if used too frequently.

TEACHING ABOUT SIMPLE SENTENCES

BEFORE THE LESSON

Focus on really defining for pupils what simple sentences are. Plan activities that show the range of simple sentences – some of which can be very short ('I am alone.') and others longer ('I am here alone tonight in the dark, creepy house on the estate.'). Simple sentences aren't, in other words, just a matter of length.

ACTIVITIES TO BUILD THIS CONFIDENCE

Get pupils actively exploring ways of expanding simple sentences – for example, through collaborative starter activities. Some examples:

- Pupils might look at the way simple sentences create order and clarity in instructions – for example:

  First clean up the fish. Put it to one side. Mix the flour, salt and pepper together in a bowl. Add a pinch of cayenne pepper.

- They might look at the way simple sentences build tension in fiction – for example:

  He waited. There was nothing there. Where were they? Why were they late? He listened. Again, there was no sound.

- They might explore the use of simple sentences at the start and end of paragraphs – for example:

  Macbeth begins as a hero. Although later in the play we will see his dark and merciless acts, at this stage in the play he...

- They might experiment with ways of expanding simple sentences using adjectives, adverbs and prepositional phrases – for example:

  Macbeth is a hero.

  Macbeth is a <u>brave and worthy</u> hero (added adjectives).

  Macbeth is <u>initially</u> a hero (added adverb).

  Macbeth is a hero <u>at the start of the play</u> (added prepositional phrase).

All of these remain simple sentences, but each has been modified in a different way.

TEACHING ABOUT COMPOUND SENTENCES

The simplest way to link simple sentences together is to use a coordinating conjunction (like 'and' or 'but}). This is what most immature writers would do.

> **The dog barked <u>and</u> the baby woke up <u>and</u> the dog whined.**

We now have three clauses that are linked. Each clause is still a main clause and can stand independently of the others. Sometimes, when the subject of two or more clauses is the same, you can remove the second subject.

> **The dog barked <u>and</u> the dog whined.**

> **The dog barked <u>and</u> whined.**

In a compound sentence, the clauses on either side of the conjunction have equal weight: they are both main clauses. These coordinating conjunctions do not suggest that one clause is subordinate to the another.

Coordinating conjunctions include:

And

But

Or

Sometimes these may be used with other linking words:

> **And so . . . and yet . . .**

> **Not only . . . but also . . .**

You need to know:

> **What a compound sentence is; and its effect in different texts.**

Too many compound sentences can feel uncontrolled and repetitive. They link ideas together easily, but can become rambling. They characterise the work of C/D borderline pupils who will benefit from exploring the effect of combining compound with simple sentences.

TEACHING ABOUT COMPOUND SENTENCES

BEFORE THE LESSON

You will want pupils to become aware of what compound sentences are, so that they are a conscious part of their grammatical toolkit. I recommend that you explicitly explore the conventions, and then keep looking at them in the context of text types. There are examples below.

EXPLORING THE CONVENTIONS

You might give pupils a sequence of simple sentences and ask them to think about the effect of them in a text – for example:

> **The dog barked. It woke the baby. He cried a lot. The noise throughout the house was terrible. Then he fell asleep. It was quiet again.**

To make compound sentences pupils could use 'and', 'but' and 'or'.

Using OHPs, different groups might explore the impact of creating long or short compound sentences, then comparing the effect of the variety – like this:

Group A: add three coordinating conjunctions:

> **The dog barked. It woke the baby <u>and</u> he cried a lot <u>and</u> the noise throughout the house was terrible. Then he fell asleep <u>and</u> it was quiet again.**

Group B: add four coordinating conjunctions:

> **The dog barked <u>and</u> woke the baby <u>and</u> he cried a lot <u>and</u> the noise throughout the house was terrible. Then he fell asleep <u>and</u> it was quiet again.**

Group C: add five coordinating conjunctions:

> **The dog barked <u>and</u> woke the baby <u>and</u> he cried a lot <u>and</u> the noise throughout the house was terrible <u>and</u> then he fell asleep <u>and</u> it was quiet again.**

Encourage pupils to look at compound sentences in stories (children's stories sometimes use them for a reassuring effect: 'He looked and he looked, but there was no one there. He waited and waited. Again – nothing.') and in their own writing, where using simple sentences as a contrast will probably sharpen up their style.

TEACHING ABOUT COMPLEX SENTENCES

Complex sentences contain a main clause, plus one or more subordinate clauses. The main clause carries the main information of the sentences. The subordinate clause conveys background or less important information. There are various ways of creating complex sentences and this is a simple checklist of three main types:

1   Using subordinating conjunctions

Simple subordinators (= one word)	Complex subordinators (= more than one word)	Correlative subordinators (= pairs of words)
although, unless, because, while, so, whereas	in order that, in case, assuming that, so that, as long as	as . . . so; if . . . then

Although he was hungry,   **he didn't eat a thing.**
subordinate clause = background information   main clause
He hid the money   **so that he wasn't caught.**
main clause   subordinate clause

2   Using relative pronouns: 'who', 'which', 'that',

The fields, <u>which were covered in dew</u>, shimmered in the sunlight.

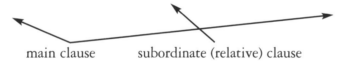

      main clause   subordinate (relative) clause

The woman entered the room, <u>which was full of her enemies</u>.

      main clause   subordinate (relative) clause

3   Using -ing and -ed verbs

<u>Walking down the street</u>, I noticed someone was following me.
subordinate clause   main clause

She watched from the window, <u>hoping she was safe</u>.
main clause   subordinate clause

<u>Frustrated by his lateness</u>, she went home.
subordinate clause   main clause

He turned up, <u>delayed by a security alert</u>.
main clause   subordinate clause

TEACHING ABOUT COMPLEX SENTENCES

BEFORE THE LESSON

Teaching complex sentences is one of the most important aspects of grammar you can work on with your pupils. It has the capacity to improve their writing significantly. However, once again it isn't a quick hit. You will need to explore the different ways of creating complex sentences, to demonstrate how they work, to give pupils opportunities to practise, and then to start bedding their knowledge into their own writing.

EXPLORING THE CONVENTION

Give pupils simple sentences and get them experimenting with ways of linking any two or three of them:

> **The weather was cold. I went out on my bike. I thought about yesterday. I wanted to forget what had happened. I rode fast. I was late. I noticed someone behind the hedge. I pedalled faster. I stopped.**

You might give one group a list of subordinating conjunctions ('because', 'although'). Another might experiment with using relative pronouns ('who', 'which', 'that'). Another might try out linking clauses with -ing and -ed verbs.

The key is to emphasise the collaborative nature of this. Keep the tone light and experimental. If a pupil writes 'Although the day was cold, I went out on my bike', explore the effect of switching the clauses round: 'I went out on my bike although the day was cold'.

WRITING

It will be important to encourage pupils to experiment with complex sentences in their next major piece of writing. You might ask them at the start of the work to write down a target – for example:

- To use a combination of simple, compound and complex sentences
- To use three different complex sentences on the first page

Before they then hand in their work, ask pupils to highlight these in the margin or to underline three or four examples of complex sentences they have used. This will encourage them to think explicitly about the knowledge and skills they are developing.

THEORY

TEACHING SUBORDINATION AND COORDINATION

I am including this topic because it sometimes helps to reinforce the key differences between compound and complex sentences. You might therefore use the spread simply to reinforce your own understanding. Equally, it might help pupils who are struggling to grasp the concepts.

COMPOUND SENTENCES

Compound sentences are made up of clauses that are coordinated. This means that they are linked together with each clause having equal weight – like this:

> I enjoy swimming and I enjoy jogging but I dislike cycling.

Clauses are linked by coordinating conjunctions:

> And
>
> But
>
> Or

COMPLEX SENTENCES

Complex sentences are made up of a main clause and one or more subordinate clauses. One way that clauses are linked is by use of subordinating conjunctions. A list of these, organised by areas of meaning, is printed on the opposite page and would be useful to have on display in your classroom. Subordination is achieved in other ways too, and the sentences below show a range of examples.

To reinforce the difference between coordination and subordination, think about the main clause in a complex sentence: this provides the main information. The subordinate clause(s) provide the background information. In the examples below, the subordinate clauses are underlined:

> She wandered into the room, <u>although she felt nervous</u>.
>
> <u>Because he was so untidy</u>, his room was a mess.
>
> <u>Still eating his toast</u>, he set off for work.
>
> The carpenter, <u>who arrived 15 minutes late</u>, looked flustered.
>
> <u>Flattered by her attention</u>, he chatted for far too long.

TEACHING SUBORDINATION AND COORDINATION

BEFORE THE LESSON

Remember that we want pupils to have a practical working knowledge of compound and complex sentences. Knowing about coordination and subordination is important because it will help many pupils to understand better the differences between the two sentence types and then (this bit is crucial) to write with more variety and flair.

STARTERS

Teach the convention – that coordination joins clauses with equal weight, while subordination creates main clauses and subordinate clauses. Pupils will only truly 'get' this through seeing examples and spotting main and subordinate clauses for themselves. Don't make a meal of this. Just use a sequence of starters to keep building their knowledge and reinforcing the skills.

DISPLAY

Pupils will also benefit from having their attention drawn explicitly to the range of subordinating conjunctions. Use them for starter activities – getting different groups using different categories of subordinators – and make sure a list like this one is clearly on display in your classroom.

Area of meaning	Subordinating conjunction	Example
Comparison	as if, as though, like	He looked at me as though he liked me.
Concession	although, though, if, even if, whereas	Although she irritates me, I still like her.
Condition	if, unless, in case, as long as, supposing	Supposing you were given the money, what would you do?
Contrast	whereas, while, whilst	I enjoy chess, whereas you don't.
Exception	except	I like cooking fish, except I often get it wrong.
Place	where, wherever	You can eat wherever you want.
Preference	rather than, sooner than	I'll stay here rather than go home.
Proportion	as . . . so, the . . . the	The more I see of him, the less I like him.
Purpose	to, in order to, so as to	I speeded up to get there on time.
Reason	to, in order to, as	I switched the computer off as it was overheating.
Result	so, so that	I turned the volume up so that I would drown out their noise.
Similarity	as, like	I'm staying here today as I feel comfortable.
Time	after, as before, since, until, when, while	He turned up after you had gone.

TEACHING ABOUT EXPANDING NOUNS AND NOUN PHRASES

WHAT YOU NEED TO KNOW

Nouns are vital elements in texts because they carry the weight of meaning. Take a sentence like this:

> At the <u>supermarket</u> I will buy some <u>cheese</u>, a <u>cauliflower</u>, <u>ice cream</u> and a <u>carton</u> of <u>soup</u>.

The nouns are conveying the main message of the sentence. We normally talk of:

- <u>Concrete nouns</u> (things we can usually see and touch, such as 'table' and 'phone'. They usually preceded by determiners (for example, 'the') and take plural endings (-s).

- <u>Abstract nouns</u> (concepts, such as 'peace' and 'idealism').

- <u>Proper nouns</u> (names of people, places and products, such as 'Manhattan', 'Lemsip'. They are not often preceded by a determiner (for example, 'the Manhattan') or a plural form ('Manhattans').

A <u>noun phrase</u> has the noun as its 'head' but may have other elements to premodify or postmodify it.

PREMODIFICATION

- The supermarket (head = <u>supermarket</u>, premodified by the determiner <u>the</u>. Other determiners include 'a', 'an', 'some', 'my', 'his', 'her', 'your', 'their', 'its').

- The untidy supermarket (head – <u>supermarket</u>, premodified by the determiner <u>the</u> and the adjective untidy. Other adjectives include 'large', 'blue', 'elegant').

POSTMODIFICATION

- The supermarket on the high street (head = <u>supermarket</u>, postmodified by a prepositional phrase, which is a phrase beginning with a preposition such as 'in', 'under', 'at', 'by', 'through').

- The supermarket that I visited (head = <u>supermarket</u>, postmodified by a relative clause which starts with 'that', 'who' or 'which').

- The supermarket illuminated by neon signs (head = <u>supermarket</u>, postmodified by a non-finite clause, meaning a clause that cannot stand on its own).

Pupils don't need to know the details of this. But they do need to know how to expand noun phrases, as this skill will add variety, texture and precision to their writing.

TEACHING ABOUT EXPANDING NOUNS AND NOUN PHRASES

BEFORE THE LESSON

Be clear why this is worth teaching. Nouns carry important weight in sentences: they tell our readers and listeners a lot about the topic. Sometimes pupils, writing would benefit from greater detail and this is often more efficiently and stylishly done by expanding the noun phrase rather than writing additional sentences.

It might be clearest to demonstrate this to pupils like this:

Expanding the noun phrase	Using separate sentences
We walked to the battered old car parked down the alleyway.	We walked to the car. It was old and battered. It was parked down the alleyway.

CLARIFY THE CONVENTION

The clearest way to demonstrate the convention is to take a simple noun phrase and to get pupils thinking about what they could add before it (premodification) and after it (postmodification) – like this:

Determiner		Noun		
The		hotel		
	haunted old dilapidated abandoned		Prepositional phrases:	on the road, in the woods, under the starlit sky
			Relative clauses:	which is shut, that looks revolting
			Non-finite clauses:	situated by the river, raided by the police, falling slowly apart

EXPLORING EFFECT

The approach here needs to be collaborative and experimental. Get pupils exploring how many adjectives can premodify a noun before it feels unwieldy (for example, the old dilapidated haunted house). Note also that adjectives can be premodified by adverbs (for example, the very/really/terribly old house).

TEACHING THE PASSIVE AND ACTIVE VOICE

WHAT YOU NEED TO KNOW

This is an area of grammar that will help your pupils to write in an appropriate style. It isn't only relevant in English. It is also especially useful in subjects such as science, where the distinction between the passive and active voice is often important.

The difference between the active and passive voice is perhaps best illustrated by these two examples:

Active: British surgeons yesterday performed a major heart transplant operation.

Passive: A major heart transplant operation was yesterday performed by British surgeons.

The passive voice shifts the agent of a clause to the end, making it seem less important. In some forms of writing this is seen as useful: it places emphasis on what happened, rather than who did it.

In most writing we are happy to make the agent of a sentence active. But in some types of writing there is a tradition of using the active voice – for example:

Active: We added potassium to the test tube.

Passive: Potassium was added to the test tube.

In an example like this, the 'agent' (we) is unimportant. The main information is what happened. However, pupils should be taught also to be wary of the passive voice, as in this example:

Passive: It was announced yesterday that asylum seekers will be subjected to more stringent tests.

This begs the question of who announced it.

Pupils need to be aware of the impact of passive forms, and be familiar with how to create them.

TEACHING THE PASSIVE AND ACTIVE VOICE

BEFORE THE LESSON

Be clear about why you are teaching the active versus the passive voice. It's relevant in the context of formal, scientific writing and it would be a wasted opportunity to teach it in other situations.

EXPLORING THE CONVENTION

Get pupils to compare the difference between the active and passive voice, using examples like this:

Active	Passive
Scientists have discovered traces of ice on the surface of Mars.	Traces of ice have been discovered on the surface of Mars (by scientists).
The government is seeking a peaceful end to the dispute with fox-hunters.	A peaceful end to the dispute with fox-hunters is being sought (by the government).
I put magnesium into the flame.	Magnesium was added to the flame.
I damaged your car.	Your car has been damaged.

Get pupils to think about the rule about how we make the active into the passive voice. What happens to the person who 'did' the action? Why do you think people use the passive form in some contexts?

Then emphasise the conventions of changing the active to the passive form. It is formed like this:

- Shifting the subject to the end and adding 'by'
- Shifting the object of the active verb to the front of the clause
- Replacing the active verb with a form of the auxiliary verb ('be') followed by an -ed participle

Then explore its effects:

- The passive form is often more wordy than the active voice.
- It can leave the reader confused.
- It often leaves out who the agent was (which can make the meaning more economical, or it can obscure meanings).

TEACHING ABOUT TENSES

PLANNING

You should aim to keep this topic simple. Most pupils will use tenses effectively in most of their writing. Tense is probably best explored by looking at it in the context of different text types. As always, aim to link reading to writing, so that, while pupils might look at a writer's choice of tense in, say, a novel or leaflet, they then actively explore the convention in their own writing.

TEXT TYPES

Encourage pupils to discuss tense in texts they are reading. Draw attention to some conventions:

Text type	Prevailing tense
Explanation (how or why something works or happens)	Present ('Hurricanes are powerful winds') or past ('Their weapons were stronger')
Information (non-chronological)	Present ('Rats are rarely more than 3 metres away from us')
Analysis (including essays)	Present ('Lady Macbeth takes matters into her own hands')
Persuasion	Present ('Another reason for banning fishing is...')
Evaluation	Past for the description of the process ('First we developed the materials'); present for the reflection ('Overall I am pleased with...')
Instructions	Present ('Start by removing the old tyre')
Recount (chronological report)	Past ('First we spend some time planning the project...')

Get pupils experimenting. Try writing stories and other texts in a different tense. Switch a fairy tale (for example, *Little Red Riding Hood*) from the past to present tense. Get pupils discussing the effect. Sometimes the present tense might add vividness to writing – as in monologues and drama.

EXPRESSING THE FUTURE

Generally, pupils need to know that there isn't a future tense in English. However, they do need guidance on how to express ideas in the future. See the next unit on teaching modals and conditionals.

TEACHING ABOUT TENSES

Tense is the time when an action takes place. People traditionally refer to past, present and future, though (as you will see) it isn't quite so simple. Pupils need an active knowledge of tenses. We aren't trying to train them simply to be able to look at a text and specify what the tense is. Rather – as the Framework for Teaching English says – pupils should be taught to:

• Keep tense usage consistent, and manage changes of tense so that meaning is clear (Year 7)
• Explore the effects of changes in tense, for example, past to present for vividness (Year 8)
• Recognise and exploit the use of conditionals and modal verbs when speculating, hypothesising or discussing possibilities (Year 8)

ESSENTIAL KNOWLEDGE

Present tense	The <u>simple present</u> uses the base form of the verb which only changes in the third person by adding -s: **I think/you think/she thinks** There is also a <u>present continuous</u> form: **I am thinking**
Past tense	The <u>simple past</u> is created by adding -ed to the base of regular verbs: **I hope – I hoped** There are also various <u>irregular</u> forms: **I drink – I drank** **I think – I thought** **I go – I went** There is the <u>past continuous</u>: **I was going** The <u>present perfect</u> enables us to refer to things at an unspecified time: **I have seen the film.** **I had been there before.** The <u>present perfect continuous</u>: **I have been waiting here for hours.**
Describing the future Most grammar experts agree that there is no future tense in English. This is a bit of a technicality – unlike French we don't have a verb ending which shows the future. Instead we use verbs forms like 'will', which are actually present tense forms: There are a number of ways in which we talk about the future:	Will/shall: **I will go. I shall be pleased.** Be going to: **I am going to eat.** Modals: **I may be going.** **I might be going.** **I shall be going.** Conditional: (This expresses hypothetical situations) **If the weather is nice, I walk to work.** **When it rains, I take the train.** **If you were invited, you should go.**

TEACHING ABOUT MODAL VERBS

Although this is (relatively speaking) a tiny area of grammar, it is explicitly listed in the English Framework:

- Recognise and exploit the use of conditionals and modal verbs when speculating, hypothesising or discussing possibilities (year 8).

ESSENTIAL GRAMMAR

You need to know what a modal verb is. You do not, however, need a detailed knowledge of the different modal categories (although they are included here for reference).

Modal verbs are special verbs which behave very differently from normal verbs. We use them to express meanings about permission ('you may'/'you can'/'you must') and possibility ('you could'/'you will').

COMMON MODAL VERBS

Can	Ought to
Could	Shall
May	Should
Might	Will
Must	Would

Modal verbs have some unusual grammatical features:

- They do not take -s in the third person – for example, 'He can talk well' (not 'He cans talk well').
- They cannot usually be used in the past tense – for example, 'She must have studied hard' (not 'She musted study hard').
- They take 'not' to create a negative – for example, 'You must not do that' (compare it with 'You eat not that').

Modal verbs are associated with authority and control. Traditionally there was a distinction between 'can' and 'may':

You can swim = you have the ability to swim.

You may swim = I am giving you permission to swim.

TEACHING ABOUT MODAL VERBS

CREATING A CONTEXT

It really is pretty pointless to teach pupils about modal verbs out of context. The aim is for pupils to use them accurately, not to be able to spot them. They therefore lend themselves to the context of certain text types:

Recounts	I **could** see the shore. I **should** have known there was a problem.
Instructions	You **must** keep a close eye on the tyre pressure. You **may** notice some vibrations.
Explanations	People **must** have known that this was wrong. There **may** be other explanations.

COMPARING MEANINGS

One of the best ways for pupils to explore modal verbs is by comparing the meanings of different sentences. They need to do this in small groups and be given time to articulate meanings – some of the expressions of tense are harder to describe than to understand.

So you could give pupils groups of related sentences and ask them to explain what the meaning or context for each one is. Sometimes it may be easier to think up a preceding or subsequent sentence to explain the meaning:

Group A

(a) I could play on the computer.

(b) I could be playing on the computer right now .

(c) I could have played on the computer yesterday.

(d) I could have been playing on the computer.

Group B

(a) The room should be tidied every day.

(b) The room should be being tidied now.

(c) The room should have been tidied yesterday.

(d) The room should have been being tidied.

WRITING

It is important that pupils get to practise using modals in an appropriate writing context. Using the sequence for teaching writing, you will want to explore modals in context and then, through shared composition, give pupils opportunities to write sentences and paragraphs of, say, an explanatory text or instructions so that they master the skill before working on the full-length assignment.

TEACHING ABOUT CONDITIONALS

The Framework for Teaching English says that pupils should:

- Recognise and exploit the use of conditionals and modal verbs when speculating, hypothesising or discussing possibilities (Year 8).

Conditionals can seem a rather abstract area of English at first, but in fact they merit further study. We use them commonly in daily conversations and more explicit knowledge will help pupils to express hypothetical ideas with more precision.

ESSENTIAL KNOWLEDGE

There are two kinds of conditional: real and unreal. Real conditional describes real-life situations. Unreal conditional describes unreal, imaginary situations.

PRESENT REAL CONDITIONAL

We use the present real conditional to talk about real-life situations. We use either 'if' or 'when'. Using 'if' suggests that something happens less frequently. Using 'when" suggests that something happens regularly.

- <u>If</u> the weather is nice, she walks to work.
- <u>When</u> the weather is nice, she walks to work.
- <u>If</u> I finish my work early, I take the dog for a walk.
- <u>When</u> I finish my work early, I take the dog for a walk.

PRESENT UNREAL CONDITIONAL

We use the present unreal conditional to talk about imaginary or hypothetical situations. The conditional clause begins with 'if' to signal that it's a hypothetical thought (namely not something that will definitely happen). In formal speech and writing, the verb form 'was' is sometimes changed to 'were':

- <u>If</u> she was thinking straight, she would say no (in formal contexts some writers might say: <u>If</u> she were thinking straight, she would say no).
- <u>If</u> I had the cash, I would travel to Egypt.
- I would buy that computer <u>if</u> it was cheaper (in formal contexts some writers might say: I would buy that computer <u>if</u> it were cheaper).

Notice that you can often switch the order of the two clauses around:

> **She would say no <u>if</u> she was thinking straight.**

TEACHING ABOUT CONDITIONALS

BEFORE THE LESSON

This is another area of grammar that needs to be taught at the appropriate point in your scheme of work. Pupils will benefit from learning about it when they are writing about relevant topics. In English, these might include assignments like these:

- Some people spend a lot of time and money on expensive adventures, such as round-the-world balloon races. Do you think these are a sensible type of challenge?
- 'This House would scrap school uniform'. What are the arguments for and against this statement?
- What would be in your election manifesto if you were Prime Minister?
- How does Macbeth change from hero to villain?

TEACHING APPROACH

Each of these texts contains a hypothetical element, which requires use of conditionals. Pupils would benefit from encountering some sentence kick-starters, like these:

> **If people didn't undertake challenges, . . .**
>
> **If there were no school uniform, then . . .**
>
> **If I had the power to make major decisions, I would start by . . .**
>
> **If Macbeth had not met the witches, he might not . . .**

- Encourage pupils to think how these sentences might continue.
- Get them to play around with the sentences, changing the sequence so (for example) the conditional clause follows the main clause (for example, life would be simpler if there were no school uniform). As always, get them to explore the effects of these changes.
- Get them to see whether there are ways of exploring hypotheses without using 'if'.

REFLECTION

The main aim is to build pupils' confidence in using this grammatical tool, and to be able to reflect on how and when conditionals are appropriate. That is why the investigative approach – exploring language, collaborating, focusing on effect, reflecting on our own learning – is so central to success.

SUMMARY

Based on this unit, you should be more confident about:

- Sentences
- Clauses
- Sentence types
- Tense
- Modal verbs
- Conditionals
- Nouns and noun phrases
- The passive voice

Remember that the idea is to build pupils' confidence through frequently returning to the topics, and always to explore it in a meaningful context. Don't bother with the passive if you aren't doing some work on newspaper styles or scientific writing. One of the things we've learnt in recent years is that grammar teaching needs to take place in a genuine context, not as some artificial self-contained activity.

If there are areas of the English Framework that you still feel uncertain about, look at the glossary. This provides further guidance on areas of grammar relevance. If you are still insecure, follow the reading lists at the end. These will lead you to other sources of explanation.

Punctuation

INTRODUCTION

Be clear about punctuation. Some of us were taught at primary school that it was there to help us know when to breathe. Not so. Pity the poor asthmatic who encounters a heavily punctuated text.

Instead, it's important to present punctuation as an essential way of supporting meaning (rather than breathing). We use punctuation to guide the reader to understand what we mean.

This section covers the basics of full stops. If your pupils can't master these, don't press on too far. Being able to delineate sentence boundaries is an essential element of being a successful writer, so expect to keep returning to the critical role of full stops.

Other punctuation marks help us to express our thoughts and ideas with greater clarity and subtlety.

Remember: none of this needs to be taught through a dreary succession of punctuation exercises. Be careful though. If you learnt to ride a bike or to drive, then chances are you broke the process into discrete skills and practised them. It's quite legitimate from time to time to have a blitz on full stops or apostrophes, for example, in a sequence of planned starters – and this will build pupils' confidence and understanding. What we don't want is unrelated exercises that do nothing but allow us to tick a box marked full stops or apostrophes.

Work on punctuation can be hugely liberating for pupils, helping them to bring shape and meaning to their ideas. Don't underestimate the importance of teaching it explicitly.

THEORY

TEACHING FULL STOPS

Full stops are, without doubt, the most important part of punctuation for your pupils to learn. Full stops show the boundaries between sentences. Without these, pupils will not be able to write grammatically.

Yet many grammar books hardly mention full stops. They take it for granted that everyone can use them accurately. In fact, throughout their learning you will need to keep paying attention to your pupils' use of full stops.

There are likely to be two main issues:

Forgetting to use full stops, so that you get sentences like this:

> **I walked down the hill my friend was waiting for me.**

Using commas where full stops are needed (called the comma splice):

> **I walked down the hill, my friend was waiting for me.**

Pupils will benefit from:

- Being reminded that punctuation is about demarcating meaning, not helping readers to take breaths or add pauses.

- Hearing texts read aloud and being required to follow them on the page, so that they see the importance of full stops (and other punctuation marks) in shaping the reader's understanding.

- Activities that help them to realise that short sentences are legitimate and acceptable. They sometimes assume that short sentences have to be separated by commas. Demonstrate that this is unnecessary. Give them plenty of examples of short sentences.

There are other uses of full stops, such as signifying abbreviations (for example, 'i.e.'), though this is becoming less common, and in ellipsis (...). But these are side issues until pupils are fully confident in using full stops to demarcate sentences. For now, focus on that.

TEACHING FULL STOPS

BEFORE THE LESSON

Remember that principles of grammar often need teaching and re-teaching. Don't assume that ten years of literacy hours and red-ink corrections will have necessarily established unerringly accurate use of full stops. Use starter activities to reinforce the legitimacy of short sentences, separated by full stops. Be prepared to ban commas for a week or two in order to emphasise the role of full stops and to eradicate comma splices.

TEACHING ACTIVITIES

Definitely avoid setting lots of dreary punctuation exercises. Life is too short. Instead, explore sentences in context.

Use a sequence of starter activities to explore short sentences – for example, in fiction writing that aims to build suspense:

> **It was cold. I was alone. I turned. I watched. I waited. Someone was behind me.**

Ask pupils to make up their own eight-sentence suspense stories. Each sentence has to be short and separated from the next only by a full stop.

Or focus on instructions. Get one pupil to leave the room while others think of a route that he or she must follow around the classroom, rather like a programmed robot. Pupils should come up with a sequence of brief, one-sentence-long instructions, like this:

> **Turn 90 degrees right. Walk to the large desk. Stop. Turn 90 degrees left. Take five paces forward. Pick up the board marker. Walk forward to the board. Write your name.**

Pupils love this game. It tests the precision of their instructions and reinforces the legitimacy of short sentences (and, therefore, the importance of full stops to demarcate sentence boundaries). To make it more interesting, get the pupil reading the instructions to face the wall so that he or she can't see what the 'robot' is doing. This leads to greater hilarity when instructions go wrong. For particular excitement (though I take no responsibility for the consequences with certain groups), blindfold the 'robot'.

LEARNING REVIEW

- Get pupils to summarise the key function of full stops.
- Get them to collect examples of short sentences from a range of genres. Get them to annotate and display these around the classroom.
- In setting up essays, discursive writing and factual writing, remind them of the clarity simple sentences can bring to the start and end of paragraphs. In the process, reinforce the impact of full stops.

TEACHING COMMAS

One of the most useful jobs you might do for your pupils is to impose a temporary ban on commas. Use of the comma splice – deploying a comma to separate sentences where a full stop (or colon or semi-colon) is needed – is an indication of someone who hasn't quite got a grasp of sentence control.

Here is an example:

Comma splice version	Punctuated with a full stop, semi-colon or colon
I was late, I arrived around 8 o'clock.	I was late. I arrived around 8 o'clock. OR I was late; I arrived around 8 o'clock.

You can see why someone might be tempted to use a comma splice. The subject of the two sentences is the same ('I') and using a full stop can feel too strong, too intrusive.

So what are commas for?

1   They separate items in a list:

Between words: **I will buy cheese, ham, potatoes and milk.**

Between phrases: **there was a carton of milk, a packet of lentils, a bottle of orange juice and a mango.**

Between clauses: **I came, I saw and I conquered.**

People sometimes wonder whether to use a comma before 'and'. As a general principle, there's no need, but occasionally a comma can be useful in showing the end of a list and the start of a new clause – like this:

I bought some cheese, ham, potatoes and milk, and then I went home.
(without the comma before the second 'and', you might assume you were still reading items in a list.)

2   Parenthetical commas bracket off self-contained words, phrases and clauses within a sentence. ('Parentheses' is the formal word for curved brackets – these commas work like brackets.)

Words: **Peter, agonisingly, watched as the train approached.**
Phrases: **Peter, in an agonised moment, watched the train approach.**
Clauses: **Peter, who should have been home by now, watched the approaching train.**

In pairs like these, commas can really add clarity to your writing.

3   To separate phrase and clause boundaries:

Waking up suddenly, he reached for the alarm clock.
In a fit of rage, he reached for the knife.

4   In speech punctuation:

This is a technical use of commas, a convention, which pupils simply need to learn. See the section on speech punctuation.

TEACHING COMMAS

BEFORE THE LESSON

It is most important for pupils to understand that commas only have the power to separate items within a sentence. In the punctuation league tables they are at the bottom, with full stops in the premiership, followed by semi-colons and colons, then commas. Used skilfully, however, they are the mark of a confident, assured writer.

Remember: teach pupils that full stops are important and short sentences quite legitimate (see the Teaching full stops section). Then show them that commas can't link sentences together. They work within sentences by separating words, phrases and clauses, but they cannot separate sentences: they simply aren't strong enough.

Don't reach for a book of punctuation exercises. Pupils need to learn about commas in the context of their own writing. Use the following teaching sequence:

TEACHING IDEAS

Use starters across a sequence of lessons to explore the conventions and get pupils practising. A good starting point, which clarifies the usefulness of commas, is to get them working on texts without commas:

> **The picture with its fresh and unexpected colours changed the way we viewed the world.**

Look at the way parenthetical commas assist the reader:

> **The picture, with its fresh and unexpected colours, changed the way we viewed the world.**

Get them generating other examples to explore three types of commas:

- parenthetical commas (red item)
- commas to separate lists (yellow item)
- commas to mark off phrases/clauses (green item)

Pupils could think up the examples (without adding the commas) and write them on to a sheet of acetate. They should then reveal their examples, one at a time. In groups, pupils hold up a colour to indicate which use of the comma is required (and get one point). For their next point they have to punctuate the example correctly.

REVIEWING THE LEARNING

Then get them to apply the same technique in the opening paragraph of a discursive or factual assignment. Get them to highlight it in their draft, or make a note in the margin.

All of this is important for the transfer of learnt knowledge to applied knowledge, and it will only happen if pupils are encouraged to build a specific feature into their own work, having previously practised it in a small unit.

Get pupils to devise a poster or sign that reminds other writers of the basic rules of commas, plus some examples.

TEACHING SPEECH PUNCTUATION

Speech punctuation has various conventions that pupils need to learn in order to write dialogue that is accurate. It is easy to overcomplicate the topic, leaving pupils bewildered. So here are five essential ingredients of speech punctuation.

1   Use speech marks around the words that a person says:

> 'Hello,' said Nicholas.
> Matthew replied, 'Hi.'

2   The start of these words will need a capital letter, unless they are continuing from an earlier comment:

> 'Are you worried?' asked Nicholas.
> 'Yes,' replied Matthew, 'but it's nothing much.'

3   The end of the spoken words will need a punctuation mark, inside the speech marks, if the sentence carries on:

> 'I saw someone outside,' said Nicholas.

4   The words after the spoken words do not need a capital letter, even after an exclamation mark or full stop:

> 'What's that?' asked Nicholas.
> 'It looks like a snake!' shrieked Matthew.

5   In introducing speech, it's conventional to use a comma:

> Nicholas said, 'I've had enough of this.'
> Matthew replied, 'Me too.'

It is useful to know that the verb that introduces or follows the spoken words (for example, 'Nicholas said' and 'replied Matthew') is called the speech verb.

TEACHING ABOUT SPEECH PUNCTUATION

BEFORE THE LESSON

Don't teach this in isolation: it won't work. Work on speech punctuation when pupils will need to demonstrate that they can use it. If they are writing a story or an extract from their autobiography, for example, then work on speech punctuation is likely to be much more effective.

TEACHING APPROACHES

I recommend that you teach speech punctuation as part of a sequence of work on dialogue. Pupils need to be confident in how dialogue in fiction works and how much to use. They should think about whether dialogue sometimes works better without speech verbs – like this:

With speech verbs	Without speech verbs
'Hello,' said Mathew.	**'So, anything to report?'**
'Hi,' said Nick.	**'Not really.'**

This gets the reader working harder – making us work out who is speaking, but without clogging up the page with lots of speech verbs like 'said' and 'replied'.

Get them also thinking about the appropriateness of dialogue. Too much dialogue can be very tedious. Exchanges like the four lines above are unlikely to enhance a story.

Once pupils have thought about the stylistic features of using dialogue, then you should focus on the conventions of writing it. To give them practice, you might copy a page from a comic (the *Beano* works well), getting pupils to retell the story by converting the words in the speech bubbles into dialogue. Give them access to the five conventions of speech punctuation by (a) demonstrating how to use it and (b) having the conventions on display somewhere.

LEARNING REVIEW

Pupils will benefit from having a reference point for speech punctuation, either in their exercise books or folders, or in a display. The conventions are definitely something that need regular practice before being fully internalised.

TEACHING SEMI-COLONS

George Orwell was famously dismissive of semi-colons. In fact, he wrote a novel (*Coming up for Air*) without using any.

I've always found semi-colons really helpful for adding shades of subtlety to writing. Somewhere between the strength of a full stop and a comma, they can separate phrases and clauses that are linked in their meaning.

Some examples:

1   Semi-colons link clauses which have the same subject:

> **I enjoy eating out; I'm also happy to stay in.**
> **The cat moved slowly across the carpet; she seemed unwell.**

Notice here that you could just as easily use the conjunctions 'and' or 'but'. That's a good way of thinking about semi-colons: use them where you might otherwise link phrases or clauses with 'and' or 'but'.

2   Similarly, semi-colons link clauses to create contrasts:

> **Macbeth begins as a hero; by the end of the play he is a villain.**
> **The lorry was approaching fast; meanwhile the car was speeding away.**

Again, notice the way the semi-colon creates balance. You could use full stops here, but the semi-colon suggests a link between the two ideas.

3   Semi-colons separate longer items in a list (namely, phrases):

> **When you get to the furniture store, you need to look for: a large, pine table that has fold-down flaps; a table lamp which emits a light that is soft, diffuse and unobtrusive; a new teapot.**

Notice how the semi-colons rein these ideas in. They give shape and control to the sentence. Commas would leave us feeling confused, uncertain where one phrase ended and another began.

TEACHING SEMI-COLONS

BEFORE THE LESSON

Don't start teaching semi-colons if your pupils haven't got a good grasp of the need for capital letters and full stops to demarcate sentences. However, many pupils are liberated by semi-colons, learning that there is a punctuation device which usefully falls between the strength of a full stop and a comma.

One teacher I knew used to tell his pupils: 'If you aren't sure whether to use a full stop or a comma, use a semi-colon.' That worked well around 90 per cent of the time. It is, perhaps, better to remind pupils that a semi-colon stands in place of conjunctions like 'and' and 'but' to link phrases and clauses together.

Then demonstrate the beauty of them. Pupils need to see you writing, demonstrating the thought processes that are at the heart of the decisions we make when composing texts. For example, you might demonstrate how you would open an assignment about relationships in *Of Mice and Men*:

You say	You write
I want my opening sentence to grab the reader's attention and to get straight into the subject, so I might write...	The novel begins with two men on the run.
I want to give some evidence and quickly show that I'm doing more than just retelling the story.	As they come out from the undergrowth into the scrubland by the pool, we see the strange partnership of...
Think of a better word than 'come out'.	As they emerge...
And here's where I need to start showing what the two characters are like. So I write a brief summary of each character. Notice the variety of sentences I use – a statement and then a question. And look at how the semi-colon lets me put the description of Lennie and George side-by-side in the same sentence.	Lennie, gigantic, powerful and childlike; George, thoughtful, responsible and irritable – two apparently different characters. What brings them together?
Here's another example.	George pauses to check the water; Lennie just dunks his head straight into the pond.
See the way the semi-colon lets me link two related ideas? Now you have a go at two opening sentences and do the same – use a semi-colon to show how you're balancing ideas.	

None of this is a quick hit. You'll want to come back to semi-colons. But the point is that pupils won't learn the technique without seeing it modelled by you.

LEARNING REVIEW

Get pupils going back to the conventions. What does a semi-colon allow them to do that a full stop or comma won't. Get them to collect some examples from essays and books (they won't find many in newspapers). Have a crib sheet on the wall – a quick reminder of what semi-colons do, a statement of their status between a full stop and comma; how they can join phrases and clauses; how they can create balance as well as contrasts; how they replace the words 'and' or 'but'.

TEACHING COLONS

Henry Fowler described the colon as:

> 'Delivering the goods that have been invoiced in the preceding words'.

Precisely! Colons work like a pair of headlamps. They point ahead to a conclusion, list or quotation. Some examples:

> From the opening line of the story, John Connolly grabs our attention: 'The bishop was a skeletal man, with long, unwrinkled fingers and raised dark veins that ran across his pale skin like tree roots over snowy ground'.

> In this speech I will make three main points: first, I will argue that fishing is barbaric; second, I will show that it is as bad as fox-hunting; finally, I will show that there are better ways of catching fish without using hooks.

> Detective Inspector Henwood suddenly saw what other officers had not noticed: the absence of a body and a weapon was a clue in itself.

In class, colons are especially useful in texts which include lists:

> Remember to pack the following: raincoat, sandwiches and a small amount of cash.

They are also essential for writing well about literature:

> Lady Macbeth is furious and determined: 'stick your courage to the sticking-place', she says.

Notice the convention that the words that follow the colon do not need to start with a capital letter.

TEACHING COLONS

BEFORE THE LESSON

Teach colons in the context of pupils' own writing. Don't teach them as an isolated 'fact you need to know about punctuation'. It will be most useful to teach them before quotations in literature assignments. I suggest you do this in the broader context of how to use quotations.

TEACHING POINTS

First, teach colons in the context of writing about literature. Here I would suggest the following teaching points:

(a)   Every point you make about a text needs to be supported by a quotation.

(b)   The best assignments use lots of short quotations embedded into the writer's own sentences. For example, 'The Chorus introduces Romeo and Juliet as "a pair of star-crossed lovers"'). Then follow up the quotation with a comment about it.

Sometimes you will want to use longer quotations. Use a colon to introduce the quotation, like this:

> **The play is full of mysterious and menacing images:**
>
> **'Come, civil night,**
> **Thou sober-suited matron, all in black.'**

Pupils could also explore the way writers use colons to build tension in their writing. (Graham Greene and Raymond Chandler are good examples.) Again, demonstrate this yourself, writing a sentence in two parts to show how the first builds up to the colon:

> **Walking up the staircase I knew that something terrible awaited me: I was not wrong.**
>
> **Stepping into the fog, Susan sensed something move: a dark shape retreated into the garden.**

These could be written as two sentences. But, like searchlights, the colons help the reader to sense that there is something ahead.

Having demonstrated the convention, get pupils writing their own suspense-filled sentences. Give them a setting (for example, an abandoned railway station, the storeroom of a supermarket, a school building at night).

LEARNING REVIEW

Get pupils to restate the convention. What are colons used for? How do they help readers in literature essays? How are they useful in lists? How do they help to build suspense in fiction writing?

THEORY

TEACHING APOSTROPHES

Apostrophes fall into two different categories: possession and abbreviation.

Apostrophes for possession	Apostrophes for compression
These indicate that something belongs to someone or something.	These indicate that the word has been shortened or compressed.
Examples: This is Wordsworth's finest poem. These are the children's toys.	Examples: It's getting very hot. (= it is) You can't be serious. (= cannot)

What you need to know:

APOSTROPHES FOR POSSESSION

To show the possessive form of a noun, simply add apostrophe + 's':

- A dog's lead
- That woman's shoes
- A day's work
- A week's wages

To show the possessive form of a plural noun that already ends in 's', just add an apostrophe after the existing 's':

- The boys' game
- The dogs' leads
- Two weeks' work

If the plural form doesn't end in 's', add apostrophe + 's' as you would for the singular form:

- The children's games
- The women's shoes

APOSTROPHES FOR COMPRESSION

The apostrophe shows where a letter has been omitted. It's as simple as that.
  Other things you ought to know:

- People sometimes get confused about 'theirs' and 'its'. 'Theirs' is a pronoun. Think of it alongside 'his' and 'hers'. 'Its' is a determiner. Think of it alongside 'his','her' and 'their'.
- Some nouns that end with 's' give you a choice of whether to add just an apostrophe or apostrophe + 's'. As a rule of thumb, if you can hear the extra 's', add it:

  Charles's appetite

  Jesus's teaching

TEACHING APOSTROPHES

BEFORE THE LESSON

It's easy to make heavy weather of apostrophes. Keep it simple and clear, using lots of lively starter activities to reinforce understanding and to build confidence. Starters are the key to teaching apostrophes because they allow you to keep it light and fast-moving. However, you will need to get pupils to understand the conventions: apostrophes for possession versus those for compression.

TEACHING APPROACHES

Demonstrate the conventions, perhaps by initially keeping possession and compression separate. Give a few examples, but time spent grinding through apostrophe exercises is usually wasted. The main areas of confusion will be:

- Plurals
- **It's/its**

The starter activity below will help to reinforce understanding of the latter.

APOSTROPHE CHALLENGE

This activity helps pupils to distinguish between some of the hardest homophones. As part of a starter activity, give pupils a sentence that contains an apostrophe challenge. Say the sentence out loud and then give pupils five seconds to think of which form of the word it is.

If you think it's this version of the word, put your hands up when I click my fingers.	If you think it's this version, freeze when I click my fingers.
They're	Their
Who's	Whose
It's	Its

Then say a sentence like this:

> **Those boys on the field – they look like they're causing trouble.**

> **Those boys say they have lost their football boots.**

> **This is the referee who's refereeing the match.**

> **At the side of the pitch the cat stretched its legs.**

Get students talking about how they worked out which form of the word to use.

Repetition of this activity over a sequence of starters really does build pupils' knowledge. The real beauty of it is getting pupils to explain to each other how they distinguish between the two homophones. Often they can explain more clearly and relevantly than we can.

SUMMARY

SUMMARY

This section should have cemented your understanding of different punctuation marks, and the role of punctuation in clarifying meaning.

It should also have given you some ideas on how to build your pupils' grasp of punctuation.

Remember: there may be times when you will want to outlaw certain punctuation marks (like commas), or to ask pupils to highlight capital letters and full stops in different colours, so that they emphasise the decisions they have made.

Punctuation is certainly an area we have to return to frequently as English teachers. But it is also an area of high impact. Help your pupils to eliminate the comma splice and move on to a more assured use of full stops and semi-colons, and you will have made a significant input into their skills as writers.

Paragraphing and Cohesion

INTRODUCTION

This is a short but important section. Many of us were taught little about how to give texts coherence – that is, how to help readers to make sense of how one idea is linked to another.

This section explores paragraphing – something pupils will genuinely benefit from. They need to know how to open and close paragraphs, and how to use various techniques to make links across paragraphs.

The unit also covers other aspects of cohesion – how as writers we may bring order to texts.

There are various active ways to explore this:

- Cutting up texts and getting pupils to re-order them

- Getting pupils to link, with lines or highlights, the cohesion created through tense or pronouns

- Getting pupils to rewrite texts to explore the way they link together

Remember that different texts will have different conventions. A tabloid newspaper uses short sentences and subheadings to create cohesion. An academic essay or technical magazine article may use a different approach.

It is important, therefore, that pupils explore texts from a range of contexts, looking not only at what they say, but at how they are held together.

TEACHING PARAGRAPHING

For those of us who are effective language users – and as teachers we are all effective users of spoken and written language – it can be easy to assume that paragraphing is a simple matter. We simply start a new paragraph when we start a new topic. In fact, many pupils need more explicit guidance than this, as well as more detailed teaching about other aspects of paragraphing.

YEAR 7 PUPILS NEED TO KNOW:

- When and how to start a new paragraph, using the first sentence to guide the reader
- How to identify the main point of a paragraph and how other information relates to it
- How to explore paragraphs which contain sentences that are not ordered chronologically
- How to organise their ideas into a logical sequence of paragraphs – introducing, developing and concluding them appropriately

YEAR 8 PUPILS NEED TO KNOW:

- How to explore and compare different methods of grouping sentences into paragraphs – such as chronology, comparison or through adding exemplification
- How to develop different ways of linking paragraphs using a range of strategies – such as choice of connectives, reference back, linking phrases

YEAR 9 PUPILS NEED TO KNOW:

- How to evaluate their ability to shape ideas rapidly into cohesive paragraphs
- How to compare and use different ways of opening, linking and completing paragraphs

Paragraphs often begin with *topic sentences* which guide the reader to the content of the ensuing paragraph. These are especially useful in paragraphs which explain, analyse and argue. 'Paragraph sprawl' occurs when irrelevant details are added in. Here are two examples of ineffective and effective paragraphs:

I think that there are too many reality TV shows on television. *Big Brother* exploits the people who are in the house and the producers encourage them to get into conflict. Other programmes like *The X Factor* are more interesting because they give people a chance to be famous for their talents. *X Factor* is my favourite. Part of the fun is watching the way people cope with pressure, whether of fame or of being cooped up with lots of other people.	I think that there are too many reality TV shows on television. They fall into different categories: those that focus on ordinary people in ordinary situations; those that put ordinary people into unusual situations; and those that give ordinary people a chance to become celebrities by showcasing their talents. As viewers we watch each of these to see what ordinary people are like and how they react under pressure. While this can be entertaining, it can also feel like exploitation.
This begins with a topic sentence but then too quickly jumps from one example to the next rather than developing the argument. It also contains the irrelevant sentence '*X Factor* is my favourite.'	This uses the same topic sentence and then explores the issue before looking at individual examples. Notice how semi-colons are used to present three different examples, creating a nicely balanced structure. Subsequent paragraphs might then explore each type of show in more detail, using linking phrases like 'The first type of reality show, then, includes . . .'

Because of their importance, connectives are dealt with separately in the next spread.

TEACHING PARAGRAPHING

BEFORE THE LESSON

Build paragraphing explicitly into your planning so that pupils are taught it systematically, not by chance. It might be that work on writing story openings would be one useful context – looking at how paragraphs are used in chronological writing. It is important that pupils also explore paragraphing in other text types, especially explanation and other non-chronological forms.

Teach pupils some essential ingredients of paragraphs:

- The usefulness of topic sentences to establish what a sentence is about
- How subsequent sentences in a paragraph should relate back or develop this
- The use of linking phrases, pronouns and connectives to build cohesion within paragraphs
- How a simple sentence at the end of a paragraph can add clarity to the topic

SAMPLE TEXT: ARGUMENT WRITING

To make this active, use starter activities in which pupils assemble a paragraph from ready-made sentences, like this:

- Undertaking extreme challenges to raise money is a good thing.
- Some people go trekking in the Himalayas or bungee-jumping for charity.
- While having once-in-a-lifetime experiences, participants are also benefiting other people.
- Some people criticise this kind of 'designer' fund-raising, seeing it as a gimmick.
- Why shouldn't people have fun while making money for others?
- People who do this should be applauded, not criticised.
- Extreme fund-raising is definitely a positive thing.

Get pupils playing with the order of these, deciding how they would sequence the sentences, whether any sentences are irrelevant, whether there are any linking words to add, and then – crucially – explaining their decisions. Do the same for different text types. Encourage them to use appropriate terms such as 'topic sentence' and 'connectives'.

Use plenaries to get pupils talking not just about what they have done (put sentences into a sequence) but, more importantly, what they have learnt (how to open a paragraph with a topic sentence, and how to link other sentences to it).

READING

Encourage pupils to look at paragraphs in lots of texts. Homework might be to look at a text type of their choice (newspaper article, recipe, holiday brochure) and to be prepared to talk about one paragraph: how it is structured; how the sentences relate to one another; examples of linking words and phrases.

Get pupils looking at and comparing each other's opening, continuing and concluding paragraphs. This can be done in very short bursts, but will build their familiarity with the conventions and make them into more reflective language users.

THEORY

TEACHING COHESION

Cohesion is an important principle in grammar, though many people probably haven't been taught it explicitly. It is the term to describe various ways of linking sentences and paragraphs in a text. Here is what you need to know:

Cohesive device	Quick definition	Example
Pronoun	Pronouns allow us to refer back to people, places and objects without repeating their names. As the word 'pronoun' suggests, they stand in for the noun. Pronouns include 'he', 'she', 'it', 'they', 'them'.	The pupils were late for class. <u>They</u> got in trouble. Mrs Hird visited. <u>She</u> seemed happy.
Determiners	These are words like 'a', 'an', 'their', 'his'. They tell us more about a noun (notice how much we learn from the three determiners here: 'some children', 'my children', 'their children'). They can be an important means for helping to avoid repetition.	Wynn and Sarah have brought <u>their</u> children. RATHER THAN Wynn and Sarah have brought Wynn and Sarah's children.
Conjunctions	These link phrases, clauses and sentences together. The most common conjunctions are 'and', 'but' and 'or'. Sometimes 'and' and 'but' are used at the start of sentences for emphasis.	We watched the film <u>and</u> we had an ice cream. <u>But</u> the best part was when we got back home.
Conjuncts	These are adverbials which link together clauses, sentences and paragraphs. They are one of our most important tools in teaching paragraphing. There are various categories of conjunct as you can see in the 'example' column.	Sequencing – <u>first</u>, <u>secondly</u>, <u>to begin with</u>, <u>furthermore</u>, <u>next</u>, <u>finally</u>, <u>to conclude</u>, <u>meanwhile</u> Summarising – <u>all in all</u>, <u>thus</u>, <u>to sum up</u>, <u>overall</u>, <u>altogether</u> Illustrating – <u>such as</u>, <u>unless that is</u>, <u>for instance</u> Emphasising – <u>above all</u>, <u>in particular</u>, <u>especially</u> Cause and effect – <u>therefore</u>, <u>consequently</u>, <u>as a result</u>, <u>because</u>, <u>so</u> Qualifying – <u>otherwise</u>, <u>in that case</u>, <u>however</u>, <u>except</u>, <u>if</u> Contrasting – <u>unlike</u>, <u>whereas</u>, <u>in other words</u>, <u>on the other hand</u> Comparing – <u>equally</u>, <u>in the same way</u>, <u>similarly</u>, <u>likewise</u>
Adverbials	Adverbials of time and place allow connections between different parts of a text.	Time: <u>three weeks later</u>, <u>next day</u>, <u>afterwards</u> Place: <u>at the other side of the forest</u>, <u>inside the house</u>, <u>above their heads</u>

Note also that effective writers create cohesion by their choice of vocabulary. They will choose words which don't repeat earlier words but refer to the same 'semantic field' or area of meaning: 'The knight rode through the <u>forest</u>. The <u>trees</u> were dark and menacing. The <u>wood</u> was far from welcoming.'

TEACHING COHESION

BEFORE THE LESSON

Be clear about what you want pupils to know. It's important not to overcomplicate or alienate pupils with excessive terminology. The essential information for pupils is that there are two types of connectives:

* Conjunctions (which link clauses – for example, 'and', 'but', 'because')
* Conjuncts (or connecting adverbs) which link ideas across sentences and paragraphs (for example, 'therefore', 'despite this'); you might simply want to refer to these as 'linking words'

DISPLAY

Have a definition of connectives in the classroom. Keep it simple, such as: 'the words and phrases we use to link sentences and paragraphs in a text'. Have examples of different connectives.

FAMILIARISING PUPILS

Get pupils familiar with the concept of cohesion. Some pupils will currently lack ambition in the way they write, linking clauses together using 'and' and 'but', and linking sentences and phrases with 'then'. Use starter activities to get pupils, in pairs or small groups, linking sentences in more challenging ways. Give them a number of sentences and get them to explore how they would link the ideas:

> **We warmed the chocolate in a bowl. We added the butter.**

Could become:

> **First we warmed the chocolate in a bowl. Then we added the butter.**

Or:

> **We warmed the chocolate in a bowl and then we added the butter.**

Get pupils to articulate the choices they make: 'We chose to use two connectives. They both show sequence'.

READING

Encourage pupils to pick out connectives in texts they are studying in your lesson or other subjects. Ask them to collect examples from across the curriculum. Do a survey of whether certain connectives are used more in certain subjects (for example, science subjects may use more cause and effect conjuncts).

WRITING

This is where you will make the biggest impact. Use the writing sequence to provide models of good writing. Demonstrate how you might use connectives or other devices to link ideas. Use shared composition to involve them in brainstorming alternative words and phrases.

SUMMARY

Paragraphing is something taken too easily for granted. Saying to pupils, 'Aim for three paragraphs to a page' can make us feel that we've done our bit.

This section should have demonstrated the importance of highlighting various forms of cohesion across texts. In particular the explicit teaching of connectives can make a significant difference to the quality of pupils' writing.

Language Varieties

INTRODUCTION

This section looks at texts on a larger scale, exploring some of the sociolinguistic issues such as Standard English and speech versus writing.

Don't be duped into thinking that these topics are less important, that they sound less tangible. Our pupils need to know *about* language, as well as how to use it. This section aims to address language knowledge as well as usage.

Inevitably we are dealing with some major issues here, and areas that linguists have given over to significant debate. Here you get the essentials, not the peripheral information. It will be important, therefore, if you are working on an in-depth language study with pupils, that you read around the topics in order to give them further detail. A reading list is provided on page 102.

TEACHING STANDARD ENGLISH

Whole books are devoted to defining and debating Standard English. You need to know some essential information to help your pupils use Standard English appropriately and accurately.

Linguist Sidney Greenbaum has defined Standard English as 'the variety of English that is manifestly recognised in our society as the prestigious variety'. Any controversy comes from the 'prestigious' part of this definition because some people dispute it. They point out that Standard English is a minority dialect – used by perhaps 12–15 per cent of the population – and therefore see it as based on social elitism and educational privilege.

In the classroom, this attitude is usually unhelpful. Pupils need to explore what Standard English is, how it relates to other dialects, and why it has such status. From this they will learn when using Standard English is essential, when it's appropriate, and when it doesn't matter.

A rule-of-thumb definition of Standard English:

(a) It is a dialect (a variety of English) alongside other varieties, such as Yorkshire or Geordie.

(b) It is an important dialect because it is not linked to one geographical area or social class. It also has considerable intellectual and social status and is used in the law, in education, in print, and in TV and radio (sometimes in conjunction with regional accents).

(c) Standard English is a purely social dialect. Although its origins were originally in the southeast of England, it is now used all over the English-speaking world, and not just in one region.

(d) Standard English is the dialect used for most written English forms, giving it a more permanent nature than many other dialects, as well as prestige from being the 'official' source of English.

(e) The status of Standard English derives from being selected (though not by any overt decision) as the variety to become the standard variety. It developed because it was the variety associated with the social group with the highest degree of power, wealth and prestige. This has been reinforced since because it has been employed as the variety used in education.

In the English Framework, Standard English is presented as something for pupils to explore actively – for example, using it consistently in formal situations and in writing (Year 7); being able to define how some of its grammatical features compare with other dialects (Year 8); exploring attitudes to Standard English (Year 9).

TEACHING STANDARD ENGLISH

BEFORE THE LESSON

Remember that your main aim is for pupils to write consistently using Standard English, and use it in formal situations. By Year 9, pupils will need to have a better understanding not only of the key features, but also of attitudes towards Standard English.

TEACHING APPROACHES

To explore Standard English actively you might:

- Look at extracts of regional dialect in a novel – for example, David Almond's *Heaven Eyes*, where some characters use Standard English and others do not. This will help to emphasise the differences between standard and non-standard forms. Pupils research examples of phrases and sentences they might hear spoken but would not expect to see written (except as dialogue):
  I never do nothing on Fridays. I've just ate my tea. We was out when it happened. I really likes it when Sarah comes round. The place were dead quiet.

- Create a text where we *expect* Standard English, but include some non-standard features – for example, a radio news report rewritten to contain errors of agreement and double negative:
  The Prime Minister's been in Birmingham today chatting to school children. We was hoping to bring you a live report...

- Pupils explore why this text feels inappropriate.

- Pupils explore various situations and decide whether they think it is necessary to use Standard English.

Speaking and listening	Writing
Chatting with friends before school	A letter of complaint to a company
An interview for work experience	An email to a friend

To explore the grammatical conventions, you might:
- Get pupils comparing a text in Standard English with a different dialect, looking for examples of some key differences.

Grammatical feature	Standard English	Other dialect
Subject – verb agreement	<ul><li>I am, you are, he is</li><li>I do, you do, they did</li><li>I go, you go, they went</li></ul>	<ul><li>I be, you be, he be</li><li>I do, you does, they done</li><li>I goes, you goes, they gone</li></ul>
Use of negatives	<ul><li>I don't have any</li></ul>	<ul><li>I don't have none</li><li>I ain't got none</li></ul>
Use of pronouns	<ul><li>himself, themselves</li><li>you</li><li>this/that</li></ul>	<ul><li>hisself, theirselves</li><li>youse/thee/thou</li><li>that/yon</li></ul>
Formation of past tense	<ul><li>I have seen/I saw</li></ul>	<ul><li>I have seen/I seen</li></ul>

TEACHING DIFFERENCES BETWEEN SPEECH AND WRITING

One essential part of every pupil's knowledge of English should be how speech and writing differ. The English Framework requires pupils to investigate some of the differences (for example, hesitation in speech) (Year 7) and degrees of formality in written and spoken texts (Year 8).

Bear in mind that in a multimedia age many of these distinctions are becoming blurred – take text messaging, for example. You should make your work exploratory rather than aim to define hard-and-fast rules.

A summary of the main differences between speech and writing could include:

Speech	Writing
Time-bound, transient, dynamic, part of an interactive process	Space-bound, static, permanent, usually to a distant audience
Structural features include special features: • Pauses • Repetition • Hesitation • Rephrasing • Fillers (for example, 'sort of') • Gaze, posture, gesture • Intonation and pauses to divide units of meaning	• Structured through units of discourse (sentence/paragraph) • Graphological conventions to assist the reader (capital letters, full stops, and so on) serving a similar purpose to intonation in speech
Deictic features – 'this one', 'over there' – because context-dependent	Distance means few deictic features
Often spontaneous	• Often pre-planned • Often a time-lag between production and reception
Many genres cannot adequately be represented – for example, graphs, formulas	Punctuation, capitals, colour, layout, graphological features
Informal, sometimes lower status, though in general we don't write when we can speak	More formal, status, adds authority in law and religion

You need to know about phatic language.

This is language that is used for social purposes, such as greetings. Expressions like 'Nice day' or 'How are you?' are usually phatic because they are about reinforcing a relationship between speakers rather than conveying specific meanings.

TEACHING DIFFERENCES BETWEEN SPEECH AND WRITING

BEFORE THE LESSON

This aspect of English benefits from a genuinely exploratory approach. It's definitely not about saying that writing has more status than speech; rather it's concerned with investigating the appropriateness of speech and writing in different contexts.

TEACHING APPROACHES

To explore this topic you could:

- Ask pupils to collect examples of words and phrases they expect to hear in speech (for example, greetings; fillers: 'you know', 'sort of'; hesitations: 'erm').
- Ask them to collect examples of words and phrases they would expect to find chiefly in written texts (greetings: 'Dear Sir'; formal vocabulary: 'however').
- Collect some examples of contrasting spoken/written texts on a similar theme – for example, the opening of a BBC TV weather forecast with a daily newspaper's printed forecast and someone answering the question, 'What will the weather be like today?'
- Find examples of chat show interviews; lectures; speeches; emails – that is, texts where there are less clear boundaries between speech and writing.
- Get pupils to use these to explore which features are distinctive of spoken texts (vocabulary and structures) and which are distinctive of written texts, in order to move to some generalisations about the conventions.

To compare written and spoken texts you could:

- Use a very brief spontaneous spoken text and start by demonstrating its key features:
  Oh, hi, how are you? What's that you've got? You off to Maths now or ... oh ... okay, see you later then.
- Use questions and explanation to demonstrate:
  Word level features:

    'Oh' – shows surprise

    'Hi' – informal greeting used in speech more than writing

    'How are you?' – phatic language – used as a sign of politeness/friendship rather than as a genuine enquiry

    'That' – demonstrative pronoun would make sense to the speakers, but in writing we'd need more clues what it was referring to

  Sentence level features:

    Unfinished sentence – shows how speech is less structured

LEARNING REVIEW

Get pupils converting written to spoken texts and vice versa. Get them to reflect on the changes they have made, for example, by annotating their finished text.

TEACHING ABOUT FORMALITY IN SPEECH AND WRITING

We use the term 'register' to refer to the way we vary our language according to the context. **Registers** are linked to occupations, professions or topics. A doctor, for example, will use a medical register. The formality of what she says will depend on:

- Written or spoken form
- Subject matter
- Setting
- Audience

Linguist Peter Trudgill distinguishes between register and style. Register is the vocabulary associated with a topic. Style is the degree of formality used.

This is a helpful distinction because a doctor may be using a medical register differently according to her audience. In a lecture to medical pupils, or in a journal article, her style may be formal. In explaining a diagnosis to a patient, her style may be much more informal.

Formality might show itself in more complex vocabulary, more formal sentence structures, a less spontaneous style (for example, reading prepared notes).

Sometimes speakers use **jargon**. This is use of language which often deliberately obscures the speaker's meaning.

Here are some features of unhelpful jargon:

- Vocabulary that is unnecessarily complex
- Vocabulary that is currently fashionable (buzzwords) – for example, 'interface', 'parameters', 'blue-sky thinking'
- Latin phrases (for example, 'affidavit' = statement of truth)
- Euphemisms – 'downsizing' and 'rationalising'
- Unnecessarily elaborate constructions – 'learning resource centres'

At the other end of the continuum is **slang**. This is an ever-changing set of colloquial words and phrases generally considered socially lower than standard language. Slang establishes or reinforces group identity: it can show that we belong to a group because we use fashionable words. Slang sometimes deals with taboo topics (aspects of sex, drugs, death). Some examples (relating to drink): 'blitzed', 'smashed', 'bombed', 'fried', 'hammered', 'polluted', 'toasted', 'ripped', 'slammed', 'smashed', 'wasted'.

TEACHING ABOUT FORMALITY IN SPEECH AND WRITING

BEFORE THE LESSON

Exploring formality and informality is a rich area for investigation by pupils. Think of ways to make it active – using role-play, looking at drama texts, having fun by switching the register of one context into another (for example, slang used at an interview).

TEACHING APPROACHES

To get pupils actively exploring the topic you could:

- Look at language associated with a spoken context – for example, 'Could you pass the butter?'
- Ask pupils to see how many other ways there are of expressing the same idea. They should think of examples that are sometimes informal (used for people you know well) and sometimes formal (used for people you do not know well).

    Butter!
    Excuse me, would you mind awfully if I troubled you to pass me the butter?

- You could ask pupils to draw a line to show a continuum, like this:

    Informal ←———— 1 — 2 — 3 — 4 — 5 — 6 — 7 ————→ **Formal**

- The two examples above would belong at the two extremes of the continuum.
- For each of the pupils' examples, ask them to discuss and decide where it belongs on the continuum.
- Explore this in a longer sequence, this time by composing a brief letter of complaint about a product they have bought – say, a jar of jam in which they have found a slug.
- Pupils think about how they might express the complaint face to face in a shop. Write down some of the words and phrases they would expect to use.
- Pupils plan how they would express the same idea in writing – focusing on features of vocabulary (greetings) and structures (elisions, sentence types) that would be more appropriate in a formal letter.
- Provide some sample greetings and phrases to get pupils started:

    Dear Sir or Madam/Dear Mrs Wheeler/Dear Joyce/,
    I am writing to you about... I was extremely surprised to find...
    - Pupils produce lists of other possible phrases in the appropriate register.
    - Pupils explore colloquial/formal pairings: 'ask'/'request', 'bad'/'appalling', 'upset'/'concerned'.

LEARNING REVIEW

Get pupils comparing work in progress. Read out some samples so that the appropriate tone is explored and reinforced. Get pupils making explicit the assumptions they have made and – in particular – the language decisions they have made about vocabulary and sentences. Get them giving feedback to each other about their work.

TEACHING LANGUAGE CHANGE

The English Framework does not require pupils to have a detailed knowledge of how English has developed as a language. It does, however, focus on comparing 'sentence structure and punctuation in older texts' (Year 7); recognising 'some of the differences in sentence structure, vocabulary and tone between a modern English text and a text from another historical period' (Year 8); and 'investigating ways English has changed over time and identifying current trends of language change' (Year 9).

SO WHAT DO YOU NEED TO KNOW ABOUT LANGUAGE CHANGE?

From classical languages

From **Latin**: vocabulary of learning, exploration, science: 'circumference', 'conjunction', 'compassion', 'contemporary', malnutrition', 'multilingual', 'submarine', 'substantial', 'suburb', 'supernatural', 'transfer' and hundreds more.

From **Greek**: vocabulary of science and technology, plus a surprising number of common words: 'angel', 'telephone', 'graphics', 'photography', 'scandal', 'school', 'drama', ' athlete'

From Germanic languages and French

The lexicon of Old English is almost wholly **Germanic**: 'father', 'mother', 'brother', 'man', 'wife', 'ground', 'house', 'land', 'tree', 'grass', 'summer' and 'winter'. Old English verbs include 'bring', 'come', 'get', 'hear', 'meet', 'see', 'sit', 'stand' and 'think'.

French gives us 'city', 'place', 'village', 'court', 'palace', 'manor', 'mansion', 'residence', 'domicile', 'cuisine', 'diner', 'café', 'liberty', 'veracity', 'carpenter', 'draper', 'haberdasher', 'mason', 'painter', 'plumber' and 'tailor'. In modern times many terms relating to cooking, fashion, drama, winemaking, literature, art, diplomacy, and ballet also come from France.

Other borrowings

English has acquired many words from **Spanish**. Some of these came directly into English, especially in the age of sea travel and conquest: 'armada', 'guerrilla', 'matador', 'mosquito', 'tornado'.

Italian contributes to the English lexicon in many ways. The technical lexicon of classical music is almost wholly Italian: 'allegro', 'brio', 'forte', 'piano', 'sotto voce'; 'plus 'ciabatta', 'lasagne', 'pasta'.

Common words borrowed from other languages are:

- alcohol, alchemy, algebra, sugar, syrup, zero
- hammock, hurricane, (Caribbean)
- gull (Cornish)
- howitzer, robot (Czech)
- brogue, blarney, clan (Gaelic and Irish)
- ukulele (Hawaiian)
- bungalow, jungle, pyjamas, thug (Hindi)
- paprika (Hungarian)
- ketchup (Chinese).
- bonsai, sumo, origami (Japanese)
- bamboo, orang-utan (Malay)
- lilac, caravan, chess, khaki (Persian)
- taboo, tattoo (Polynesian)
- flamingo, marmalade (Portuguese)
- mammoth, soviet, vodka (Russian)
- coffee (Turkish)
- flannel (Welsh)

TEACHING LANGUAGE CHANGE

BEFORE THE LESSON

The method of studying language change at Key Stage 3 is not to focus on historical information, but instead to get pupils actively exploring the way English has changed and keeps changing.

TEACHING APPROACHES

To get pupils actively exploring the topic, you could:

1   Ask pupils to think about slang words meaning 'good' that they use today, and then see if they can think of words with a similar meaning used by their parents or grandparents. They might come up with words like:

    • **great** • **kosher** • **fab** • **groovy** • **brill** • **wicked** • **topping** • **spiffing** • **smashing**

2   Get pupils talking about which of these words are heard today and which have fallen out of fashion. They could put them in rank order of most to least embarrrassing!

3   Explore words which have come into English from other languages by using dictionaries.

To explore language change in texts, you could:

1   Place two very short extracts of text side by side – for example, the opening of *Jane Eyre* or a verse from the King James Bible, alongside a modern version (like the Dorling Kindersley one).

2   Look at an example of a prose fiction or non-fiction text – for example, a short extract from Samuel Pepys' diary, or *Jane Eyre*. Pupils imagine it is the opening of their own story. How would they change its vocabulary and/or sentence structure for a modern audience?

    There was no possibility of taking a walk. We had been wandering, indeed, in the leafless shrubbery an hour in the morning; but since dinner (Mrs Reed, when there was no company, dined early) the cold winter wind had brought with it clouds so sombre, and a rain so penetrating, that further outdoor exercise was now out of the question.

3   Pupils compare a simplified version of a pre-1914 text, such as this modern rewrite of *Jane Eyre* (Sue Ullstein, Longman Classics).

    It was winter. The weather was very cold and it was raining. We could not go outside. I was glad; I never liked walks with my cousins, John, Eliza and Georgina Reed.

4   Pupils explore how this works, whether the effect is too oversimplified, staccato or disjointed. Why does the writer keep a semi-colon in her version? What effect does it have?

LEARNING REVIEW

To deepen pupils' understanding, get them actively rewriting a short extract of text, possibly in pairs. Take the opening of a pre-1900 text, say an extract from Pepys' diary or the first paragraph of a Dickens novel, or a Bible story. Use something that contains unfamiliar vocabulary. Pupils write an updated version for modern readers.

Get them to annotate it or create a display of their main changes. Make lists of words from other cultures, or posters of words we no longer use today. Run a sequence of starters – in the *Call My Bluff* format – in which pupils explore unfamiliar words, saying where the words come from.

SUMMARY

SUMMARY

Knowing about Standard English is an essential area of knowledge for all teachers, and for pupils. It's important to recognise its prestigious place as the overarching dialect of so many areas – education among them. The trick is for pupils to know about and use Standard English without falling into stereotypes about other dialects therefore being inferior.

Effective English teachers celebrate the diversity of our cultural and linguistic heritage. An investigative approach to Standard English, speech versus writing, and language change will help pupils to have a broader perspective on their language roots.

Many groups get interested in these topics, especially aspects of language change – topics that we might have previously reserved for A level English Language. It might therefore be worth creating a language change module as part of your core scheme of work at Key Stage 3.

Writing

INTRODUCTION

The Framework for Teaching English groups 'stylistic conventions' within sentence level objectives. I have put them as a separate writing section because of the importance of getting pupils actively exploring the conventions of different text types through writing.

Writing has traditionally been one of the weaker areas of teaching in English. We have sometimes assumed we were teaching writing when we spent time setting up a task, by giving advice about audience ('write it for a teenage reader') and narrative voice ('you could use the first person').

In fact writing is one of the most complex tasks our pupils undertake and they need various forms of intervention, guidance, challenge and support from teachers. Remember what your role is:

- Establishing a purpose and audience for writing
- Providing a model of the text
- Helping pupils to have something to say
- Giving them opportunities to develop, sharpen and revise ideas
- Encouraging collaboration
- Providing scaffolding to support their writing (from writing frames to word banks and dictionaries)
- Providing meaningful feedback

For many pupils writing can be passive and unexciting: they don't actually see the process of writing, the decision-making and rewording that goes into our final product. Therefore you'll see a strong emphasis in this section on not only providing the essential features of some key text types, but also on modelling, composing together, discussing the impact of words, phrases, sentences and paragraphs. Pupils need, in other words, to see you writing – alongside teachers of all their subjects.

TEACHING TEXT TYPES: INFORMATION

INFORMATION (NON-CHRONOLOGICAL)

Purpose: to describe the way things are
This page gives you a summary of some of the key features of the text type.

STRUCTURE (TEXT LEVEL)

- Opening statement should give a general classification, such as 'Mammals are animals with fur or hair' – followed by further technical classification if required – for example, 'Like birds, they are warm-blooded'.
- Sequence is dictated by category of information.
- Sentences giving similar information are organised in the same paragraph or series of paragraphs.
- Sections containing one or several paragraphs can be divided by headings/subheadings.
- Sections might include description of phenomena, including some or all of its qualities, parts and functions, and habits/behaviour or uses.

LANGUAGE FEATURES (WORD AND SENTENCE LEVEL)

- Usually written in present tense.
- Connectives of adding or sequencing used to join sentences or paragraphs giving similar information – for example, 'in addition', 'also', 'furthermore'.
- Connectives of comparing and contrasting used to join sentences or paragraphs giving different types of information – for example, 'compared with', 'unlike', 'in a similar manner'.
- Adjectives and adverbs used to aid categorisation.

TEACHING TEXT TYPES: INFORMATION

BEFORE THE LESSON

Traditionally, pupils are better at writing chronological than non-chronological texts. Because we read stories, watch them in films and television, tell them to one another in anecdotes and jokes, and even dream them, stories come naturally to us.

Non-chronological writing needs more attention to structure it, and pupils need lots of opportunities to write information texts. You might ask them to:

- Put together a leaflet about a subject
- Design a worksheet or fact sheet on a topic
- Describe a hobby or area of special interest

TEACHING ACTIVITIES

Use starter activities to explore the conventions, perhaps asking pupils to collect examples of similar texts and then defining their conventions. Key areas are:

Tense

Get pupils to experiment with using past and present tenses. This might vary from one section to another. Headlines are likely to be present tense, though they may not use verbs ('Mammal Facts Sheet'). The opening topic is likely to be in the present tense, but there may be a section of background information that shifts into the past tense ('The red squirrel was once noted in this area . . . ').

Connectives

Wean pupils off using 'and' and 'but' to connect ideas. Get them to brainstorm more ambitious connectives. Give them a small extract of text containing simple sentences, or ones linked with 'and' and 'but'. Get them to practise linking sentences together in different ways.

Organisation of the text

Get pupils thinking about how information might be organised. Encourage them to sketch out an overall plan of the text.

Description

Information texts need precise descriptions. Carefully chosen adverbs and adjectives will be important.

LEARNING REVIEW

Get pupils to assess their own and each other's finished information sheets. Use traffic lights or star ratings to identify areas of strength and weakness. Get them to summarise the key ingredients of this text style.

Get pupils working on small sections of the text – for example, thinking about opening paragraphs (setting the scene). Get different groups brainstorming different possible opening paragraphs and then comparing them.

Get pupils to brainstorm the relevant connectives.

THEORY

TEACHING TEXT TYPES: INSTRUCTIONS

INSTRUCTIONS

Purpose: to instruct how something should be done through a series of sequenced steps

STRUCTURE (TEXT LEVEL)

- Opening statement should indicate 'How to...'
- The text should be written in the order that events should happen (chronological order).
- The sequence could be clarified by bullet points, numbers, letters.
- Often there is a diagram or illustration.

LANGUAGE FEATURES (WORD AND SENTENCE LEVEL)

- Imperative verbs in present tense.
- Sentences should be short and each one cover one instruction only.
- Any connective words will relate to the order in which things happen – for example, 'next', 'then', 'when'.
- The text focuses on generalised human agents rather than on named individuals.
- Adjectives/adverbs are used only to be specific – for example, 'Connect the <u>brown</u> wire to the battery'.

TEACHING TEXT TYPES: INSTRUCTIONS

BEFORE THE LESSON

At the heart of writing good instructions is the need to tailor your language to the audience, clarity and precision.

Get pupils to collect examples of different instruction texts:

- Recipes
- Leaflets
- Instruction manuals
- Self-help books
- Packaging

TEACHING ACTIVITIES

Use the range of texts to draw out some general principles – the conventions of instruction texts.

Use drama to focus on the effect of imperative verbs. Get pupils to think of the commands they might give in different situations. Get them to give instructions to one another in pairs, emphasising the way imperative verbs tend to be placed at the start of sentences ('Walk four paces forward. Stop. Turn left...'). Get them to find imperative verb forms in recipe books. Compare different styles – for example, more descriptive (Nigel Slater) with more functional (Donna Hay).

Debate the appropriate format – paragraphs of instructions, bullet points, numbered instructions. What are the advantages and disadvantages of each type?

Get all pupils to write instructions on the same topic – for example, cleaning teeth – to reinforce the conventions. Compare the different styles. Draw out key learning points – for example, generalised human agents ('Add toothpaste' rather than 'You should now add toothpaste').

LEARNING REVIEW

Get pupils assessing their own and others' finished instructions. Ask another class to read them and give feedback. Give the readers a detailed summary of conventions and ask them to rate each ingredient so that feedback is specific and focused.

TEACHING TEXT TYPES: RECOUNT

RECOUNT (CHRONOLOGICAL REPORT)

Purpose: to retell events

STRUCTURE (TEXT LEVEL)

- Opening statement 'sets the scene'.
- Events are recounted in the order they occurred.
- Paragraphs are divided to show change of time, place or focus
- Text should answer the questions 'When did it happen?' 'Where did it happen?' 'Who did it?' 'What happened?'

LANGUAGE FEATURES (WORD AND SENTENCE LEVEL)

- Written in first (autobiography) or third person.
- Written in past tense.
- Connectives will relate to time, cause or contrast (see connectives chart) – for example, 'at first', 'eventually', 'because', 'whereas'.
- Focuses on individual or group participants – for example, 'we', 'I'.
- Adjectives and adverbs used to add dramatic effect.

TEACHING TEXT TYPES: RECOUNT

BEFORE THE LESSON

Recounts cover a range of styles. They might be:

- A report of an event
- An extract from an autobiography
- A factual account
- A retelling of a familiar story in a different genre (for example, a newspaper report)

TEACHING ACTIVITIES

Pupils need to think about the audience. Much derives from this – how much detail to give; what tone to use; how formal/informal to be.

In a report, the opening statement may be a topic sentence which says something about who, what, where and when:

> **A 24-year old man was arrested by West Midlands police on suspicion of robbery yesterday.**

Some recounts will aim for a more circumspect opening that aims for drama rather than factual accuracy:

> **It was supposed to be just another school ski trip to Austria. In fact, it turned into an Alpine fiasco.**

Get pupils exploring the use of descriptive writing, choosing adjectives and adverbs carefully (rather than piling up too many).

Explore different connectives in order to avoid a predictable sequence of 'then ... next day ... later'.

LEARNING REVIEW

Pupils should explore the conventions of recounts and reflect on the decisions they made in their own work. Get them to review the approach they took, commenting in specific terms on the strengths and weaknesses of their own work.

TEACHING TEXT TYPES: EXPLANATION

EXPLANATION

Purpose: to explain how or why something works/happens

STRUCTURE (TEXT LEVEL)

- General statement to introduce the topic.

- Written step by step until explanation is finished.

- Paragraphs constructed with an opening point and then further details or evidence to illustrate or support the opening point.

- Final statement sums up the main points that have been made.

LANGUAGE FEATURES (WORD AND SENTENCE LEVEL)

- Can be written in past or present tense.

- Connectives will relate to time, cause or comparison (see connectives chart) – for example, 'at first', 'from that point', 'as a result', 'similarly'.

- Use adjectives/adverbs only to be specific – for example, 'Their ships were <u>smaller</u> and <u>more manoeuvrable</u>'.

TEACHING TEXT TYPES: EXPLANATION

BEFORE THE LESSON

Explanation texts tell us how something works. Some examples:

- A science textbook explains a scientific process.
- A history fact sheet tells us why a particular event happened.
- A technology guide explains how something is built.

Notice that explanation isn't quite the same as instructions. It isn't telling us *how* to make something. It's telling us how it is made. Therefore it involves statements rather than commands ('The tanks were designed to be quickly reversed...' rather than 'Reverse your tank by...').

TEACHING ACTIVITIES

Get pupils to collect examples of explanations. Get as wide a range as possible, including internet guides and science and history books for children. Ask the school librarian to help gather sample texts. Use the opportunity to make connections with other subjects. Look, for example, at explanation texts from history or science. Get pupils to reflect on the 'hardest' topic they study in another subject and to find examples of texts which have been successful and unsuccessful at explaining the topic. What are the key features of the effective texts?

Set pupils a research project to gather examples of the conventions. Are the texts written in past or present tense? How can you tell who their audience is? What do the writers do to make their explanations clear?

Get pupils reporting back their findings, producing a checklist of key features for display. Set them a challenge – for example, explain how an internet search engine works, aimed at users who are unfamiliar with the internet.

Remember the importance of shared composition: working with the class, put together a sample paragraph, and emphasise some of its key features.

LEARNING REVIEW

Once pupils have created their own explanation text, get them to reflect on the decisions they have made. You might give them a series of opening sentences, which they complete:

Opening sentence	Explanation text
To make the design of my text clear, I decided to...	The effect of this was...
To make the explanation clear, I decided to...	The effect of this was...
With tense, I chose to...	The effect of this was...
With vocabulary, I chose to...	The effect of this was...

Also important, of course, is for pupils to get feedback on their text from a detached user. Ask pupils in a different class to review them; or involve parents in reviewing them and to fill in a checklist of strengths and areas to develop. Put together a display of the outstanding explanation texts and ask a couple of pupils to annotate the display, highlighting for all readers the essential ingredients of explanation texts.

TEACHING TEXT TYPES: PERSUASION

PERSUASION

Purpose: to argue the case for a point of view

STRUCTURE (TEXT LEVEL)

- Thesis – opening statement, for example, 'Vegetables are good for you'.

- Arguments – one per paragraph, often in the form of a point of view plus further elaboration – for example, 'They contain vitamins. Vitamin C is vital for . . .'

- Summary of main arguments and restatement of opening position, for example, 'We have seen that . . . , so . . .'

LANGUAGE FEATURES (WORD AND SENTENCE LEVEL)

- Written in present tense.

- Focus is on generic participants, not on individuals.

- Connectives are related to logic – for example, 'this shows', 'because', 'therefore', 'in fact'.

- Adjectives and adverbs are used for emotive/rhetorical effect.

TEACHING TEXT TYPES: PERSUASION

BEFORE THE LESSON

When we think of persuasive writing, it's easy to fall back on the same old genres – adverts and speeches. In fact, pupils should also critically explore other texts that are designed to persuade, like:

- Newspaper editorials
- Magazine advertorials (written to look like articles but funded by the advertiser)
- Packaging – for example, the back of breakfast cereals
- Polemical poetry
- Campaign leaflets from political parties
- Websites from charities and pressure groups

TEACHING ACTIVITIES

It might be that different groups of pupils – grouped by ability, interest, gender, or to create a mix of temperaments – each work on a different category of persuasive writing. Each group could then report back on some of the key features of the genre:

This could involve some big questions:

- How does this text try to draw the reader on to the writer's side?
- Does it address the reader directly? How? If not, why not?
- What are the main arguments the writer uses?

And here are some questions specifically exploring language features:

- What tense does the writer choose?
- What emotive words did you find?
- Which were the most important connectives for linking ideas?

Use starters and small whole group activities to work on key aspects of the text type, such as adjectives and adverbs (often important in these texts because they help to shape our emotional response). Create a paragraph of a persuasive leaflet aimed at getting pupils to eat more adventurously at lunchtime. Compose together a version without adjectives and adverbs. Then share ideas about adjectives ('healthy', 'fresh', 'delicious') and adverbs ('healthily', 'extremely', 'amazingly') that might help to make your persuasive case.

LEARNING REVIEW

Get pupils reflecting not only on what they have learnt about the text type (always going back to the conventions), but also on the role they have played in their group:

Date	My role was...	My contribution was good because...	My friend's comment was...	I could improve my speaking and listening by...
	This meant I had to speak...			

TEACHING TEXT TYPES: DISCURSIVE WRITING

DISCURSIVE WRITING – ANALYSIS INCLUDING ESSAY WRITING
Purpose: to present arguments and information from differing viewpoints

STRUCTURE (TEXT LEVEL)
- Opening statement of the issue with a preview of the main arguments.
- Each paragraph contains the statement of one argument for or against followed by supporting evidence.

Or

- Each paragraph contains one argument with some supporting evidence followed by a counter – argument and supporting evidence.
- Quotations used to support arguments/points.
- Final statement will sum up and draw conclusions from arguments made and may include writer's own recommendation or opinion.

LANGUAGE FEATURES (WORD AND SENTENCE LEVEL)
- Usually written in present tense.
- Connectives relate to logic – for example, 'however', 'therefore', 'for example'.
- Connectives relate to contrast/comparison – for example, 'whereas', 'compared with', 'similarly', 'moreover'.
- Phrases to indicate the use of evidence – for example, 'This is supported by the fact that . . .', 'this shows that . . .', 'as in . . .'
- Adjectives and adverbs will be used when value judgements are being made.

TEACHING TEXT TYPES: DISCURSIVE WRITING

BEFORE THE LESSON

Discursive writing used to be a staple of English lessons, with essay titles like 'What are the arguments for and against animal experimentation?' or 'How far do you agree that school uniform improves academic standards?' Assignments like this were useful if they introduced pupils to debating skills (something every English department should get pupils involved in).

At their worst, discursive essays can be mechanical ('In this essay I will look at the arguments for and against the topic; then I will summarise the main points and give my opinion'), so the challenge is to teach pupils to structure ideas clearly while also writing with passion and flair.

TEACHING ACTIVITIES

Sunday newspapers are full of opinion pieces. Get pupils reading them, debating, mapping out their structure, looking at how balanced (if they are), so that conventions are being hammered out.

Structure is essential to good discursive writing. There are two possibilities:

Your teaching will need to focus on some of the essential stylistic points of discursive writing: how to

Plodding	Adventurous
• Introduction • Points for the argument • Points against the argument • Conclusion	• Introduction (using quotations or facts or an anecdote to catch the reader's attention) • Argument 1 – for/against • Argument 2 – for/against • Argument 3 – for/against • Conclusion – writer's own view

use supporting evidence (for example, quotations embedded in the writer's sentences rather than pasted in as separate slabs, and always followed by further comment); active exploration of connectives (write a sample paragraph that only uses 'and', 'but', 'then', 'so': get pupils improving it); how to remain impersonal and detached, perhaps only introducing personal pronouns in the final paragraph.

REVIEW

Focus on the specific language skills that define the conventions of persuasive texts. Ask pupils to reflect on their progress in some of these areas, perhaps like this:

Skill	Progress: 1 2 3	Example
Using the introduction to grab the reader's attention, and to set out the main case		
Using connectives that signal to the reader the direction of your argument		
Using emotive vocabulary		
Supporting points with evidence		
Providing a paragraph that sums up the case		

Key to progress: 1 = not yet achieved 2 = achieved but not consistently 3 = consistently achieved

TEACHING TEXT TYPES: EVALUATION

EVALUATION, INCLUDING SELF-EVALUATION

Purpose: to record the strengths/weaknesses of a performance/product

STRUCTURE (TEXT LEVEL)

- Opening statement contains value judgement in answer to a question – for example, 'How well did your construction work?'
- Can be written in list form with bullet points, numbers or letters.
- Subheadings may be used to focus attention of writer.
- Paragraphs should contain statement of strengths or weaknesses with evidence to support statements.
- Summary will sum up strengths and weaknesses and may be followed by targets for future.

LANGUAGE FEATURES (WORD AND SENTENCE LEVEL)

- Written in first person ('I' or 'we').
- Written in the past tense to reflect on performance; present to reflect on personal/group characteristics; future for target setting.
- Connectives relate to comparison/contrast – for example, 'although', 'however', 'still', 'on the other hand' or cause and effect – for example, 'because', 'since', 'therefore', 'as a result'.
- Phrases used for commentary – for example, 'we felt that', 'it seemed as if', 'we might have', 'I thought that...'

TEACHING TEXT TYPES: EVALUATION

BEFORE THE LESSON

Evaluation is an important text type in many subjects other than English, such as science and technology. It is also, traditionally, an area of weakness, with pupils lacking sufficient guidance on how to write an effective evaluation.

To explore the text type, you could look at a range of texts that evaluate products and performances – for example:

- Newspaper and magazine surveys comparing products (*Which? M*agazine surveys; the *Independent's* weekly '50 Best' feature)
- Reviews of plays, films and music, presented in newspapers in a range of formats
- Online comparisons of different electrical products
- Examples from science and technology of pupils' evaluations

TEACHING ACTIVITIES

Pupils sometimes assume that an evaluation is all about giving an opinion. In fact, structurally, an evaluative text is likely to give 75 per cent of its space to description ('the product is...' 'the performance began with...' 'the design has various features...'), with any personal opinion towards the end ('I was impressed by...').

Structure is therefore important and pupils would benefit from seeing the overall shape of a text mapped out visually.

It might be that a good and bad model text would also help. Bad models can help us to see what to do more powerfully than good models, which can simply intimidate us with their high quality. The opening of a bad evaluation in technology would be:

> **I enjoyed making this design for a CD holder. It was a lot of fun, though I found it difficult to get started. The best bit of my design is the use of colour...**

Get pupils taking a small sample and reworking it, by making the style more impersonal by removing the personal pronouns; adding structure through subheadings, topic sentences and connectives; focusing on the product ('The design was... the colours are... the texture is...') and leaving personal commentary to the end.

LEARNING REVIEW

Reviews of performances need real audiences: get them published in a school magazine or newsletter or on a display board somewhere beyond the territory of the English department. Get pupils to comment on and annotate their own evaluations. If you have been working on evaluations for other subjects, bring in a friendly science or technology teacher and ask her to give feedback to the class, focusing on specific points of style. This sends out a powerful whole school message about the importance of reading and writing across the curriculum.

SUMMARY

This section should have shown you that there are some key areas of grammar and language knowledge that can make a powerful impact on the quality of pupils' writing. Pupils will feel confident using connectives and will appreciate different sentence types if these are taught in a specific way.

It isn't simply about what we teach, though. The section should have highlighted also an approach to writing, a teaching process, and this is modelled on the Key Stage 3 strategy approach:

- Establish clear aims.
- Provide examples.
- Explore the conventions of the text.
- Define the conventions.
- Demonstrate how the text is written.
- Compose together.
- Scaffold the first attempts.
- Independent writing.
- Draw out key learning.

Put like this, it sounds simple and utterly logical. But it's a cycle that's easy to slip out of. So keep emphasising the conventions of a text and use the process of writing to build pupils' understanding of these further, returning to the conventions at the end of the process so that pupils can demonstrate what they have learnt. And remember the importance of showing yourself as a writer: the demonstration and composing – together stages in this process are essential.

As a result, you have the opportunity to make a huge impact as a teacher: a structured approach to writing is where we can perhaps most significantly develop the skills and expression of our pupils.

Reading

INTRODUCTION

It is easy to assume by Key Stages 3 and 4 that pupils have developed all their necessary reading skills and that any further development will happen as a result of their own reading.

In fact, as teachers, we have an ongoing responsibility to help them become more confident, precise and accomplished readers – as well as giving them the foundations for a lifelong love of reading.

Pupils in school are faced with a huge range of texts, many of which are too demanding, or too undemanding, or inappropriately presented, or just tedious. One of our responsibilities, therefore, is to reflect on:

- What we give our pupils to read
- Why they are expected to read it
- How we can help them to read it

Remember that in any class – even one with a tight setting regime – you will be working with pupils with a range of reading abilities. You therefore need to:

- Develop an overview of reading
- Have strategies for making texts accessible
- Know ways of helping pupils with subject-specific vocabulary
- Know approaches that will develop explicit approaches to reading
- Actively teach research skills
- Use directed activities related to texts

Helping pupils to read more effectively is hugely liberating for them. It increases their motivation and success in learning. It also shows your commitment to a skill that needs a consistent and coherent approach across all subjects, which is something all teachers need to contribute to developing.

You therefore need:

- A systematic approach to reading
- Specific strategies for introducing texts, helping pupils to read them, helping to demystify vocabulary, and developing a range of responses

THEORY

HOW TO DEVELOP YOUR OVERVIEW OF READING

Don't take reading for granted. Some prior knowledge and systematic planning will build your pupils' confidence, help them to become better readers, and increase their motivation in your lessons.

So, make sure you have a clear view of what successful readers can do. This will help you in your planning.

Successful readers:

- Are confident in what they are doing and know how they should approach and read a text
- Recognise that texts are about much more than words on the page
- Predict what will happen next
- Ask questions of the texts
- Make links with other texts they have read both within and across various media
- Are able to relate what they read to their experience
- Pass judgements
- Evaluate text for veracity and usefulness

(*Developing Reading: Pedagogy and Practice: Teaching and Learning in Secondary Schools*, DfES)

Remember:

- It's easy to dish out texts without paying much attention to their purpose, level of difficulty, or ways of supporting pupils.
- Many pupils may assume that, with every text they are given, their job is to find the 'right' answers. Move beyond this by using texts more thoughtfully. Choose texts carefully, present them with visual interest, and use a range of activities (outlined in this section).
- Pupils will be at a range of levels in reading skills. Don't just aim for the middle of the group.

HOW TO DEVELOP YOUR OVERVIEW OF READING

See reading as an active process, not something that just happens. So:

Model the reading process . . .

Pupils should see you and others reading and responding to texts. Talk to them about the processes and strategies you use for finding specific information, getting the gist of a text, reading lengthy texts, making notes.

Prior to reading . . .

Get pupils talking about their whole process of reading with questions like this:

* Before reading, look at the title. What kind of text do you predict this is? What texts that you have already read does it remind you of? How can you tell? What type of text can you say it definitely is not? How do you know?

* Look at the first sentence or first paragraph. How has this added to your prediction of the kind of text this is? Who do you think this text might have been aimed at? Do you think it is for a general or specialist audience? How can you tell?

During reading . . .

* Give pupils sufficient time to read a text.
* Put them in reading pairs or groups. Think about grouping confident with less confident readers.
* Give them a grid or table to collect certain types of information or to record their responses.
* Get them to draw symbols, cartoons, doodles or graphs to indicate their response to different paragraphs or sections.
* Get them to use a graph to track their responses to a character's fortune or to indicate the level of tension in a story.
* Get them to record their own strengths and weaknesses in reading – how their skills are developing.

After reading . . .

* Give them time to think about their response.
* Ask fewer questions and, instead, give them an active task for building their comprehension (a summary of key points, a spider diagram, a poster), and/or synthesising and evaluating ideas.
* Get them comparing this text, its characters, themes and language, with other texts. Do this visually or using a table.
* Get them making presentations of their findings to other groups.
* Get them to set their own questions or to annotate a text.
* Importantly, get pupils talking about the processes and strategies they used for reading the text. What have they learnt about their own reading skills from this activity?

IMPROVING THE READABILITY OF THE TEXTS YOU USE

The words and sentences used by authors are obviously an important factor in how well pupils can understand the texts. When you prepare your own handouts and worksheets, you need to think about the readability of the texts.

In practice, this means considering:

- The readability of the language
- The presentation of the material

Readability of texts is usually measured in 'reading age'. A reading age of 14 years indicates a text that could be read and just understood by a pupil of 14 with an average reading age.

Although this is inevitably based on generalisations about age and ability, it is a useful indicator of the level of difficulty of texts, and a reminder of the need to have your target audience in mind.

For example:

- This short sentence needs a reading age of less than nine years.
- This longer sentence, which contains an adjectival clause and polysyllabic words, has a reading age of more than 16 years.

There are at least 200 readability tests, some of which are time-consuming to administer and interpret. However your word-processing software is likely to have a readability function. If – as in Word – this reports a reading level in terms of an American grade, it is considered normal practice to add a value of five to create a UK-based reading level.

IMPROVING THE READABILITY OF THE TEXTS YOU USE

Most important, view all texts you use from the point of view of your pupils. If you're presenting them with this text, then you want them to read and understand it. So what have you done to assist that process?

This will mean sometimes rejecting certain texts, or editing, or even rewriting them in order to ensure that they work in the classroom. You can also, of course, increase the readability of texts by paying attention specifically to layout and vocabulary (both are covered in separate spreads).

✓ Aim for:

- Accessibility – use the readability statistics tool on your word processor to investigate the language level of the text.

- Short paragraphs.

- Simple sentences at the start and end of paragraphs to help the reader to 'tune into' the topic of the paragraph.

- Connectives that clearly mark the 'direction' of a text – 'because', 'then', 'next', 'first'.

 Avoid:

- Using long complex sentences too often

- Using the passive mode where the active will do

- Using unnecessarily complicated or unfamiliar vocabulary

Here's how you might take a complicated text and improve its readability.

Before rewriting	After rewriting
Morphine, C17H19NO3, is the most abundant of opium's 24 alkaloids, accounting for 9% to 14% of opium-extract by mass. Named after the Roman god of dreams, Morpheus, who also became the god of slumber, the drug morphine, appropriately enough, numbs pain, alters mood and induces sleep. Morphine and its related synthetic derivatives, known as opioids, are so far unbeatable at dulling chronic or so-called 'slow' pain, but unfortunately they are all physically addictive. During the American Civil War, 400,000 soldiers became addicted to morphine.	Morphine is a powerful sleeping drug. It is named after Morpheus, the Roman god of slumber and is famous for numbing pain, changing our moods and making people sleepy. With its related forms (known as opioids) it is unbeatable at dulling severe pain. However, it is also highly addictive and in the American Civil War 400,000 soldiers became addicted to it. Morphine is also known as C17H19NO3 and is made from an extract of opium (a seed in poppy plants).
Reading age: 17	Reading age: 14

Edited from source: Morphine by Enrico Uva, Lauren Hill Academy, Montreal, Canada http://www.emsb.qc.ca/laurenhill/science/morphine.html

THEORY

USING LAYOUT FEATURES TO MAKE TEXTS MORE ACCESSIBLE

SPACING

Lack of spacing creates something called 'grey pages', where there is simply too much text. Readers should be able to look at a page and distinguish between headlines, subheadings, columns and captions.

Space at the top and bottom of a page is important for framing a document. Spacious side margins also encourage us to read a text. You might also consider using several columns to a page for certain texts. Long lines of small type are tiring to read because each line requires several left-to-right eye movements. On the other hand, excessively narrow columns can contain too many hyphens and therefore make comprehension more difficult.

Avoiding widows (a line starting a new paragraph at the foot of a page) and orphans (a line of continuing text at the top of a page) can also assist readers' comprehension.

Justification can also affect the readability of a text. Right justification can look attractive to the eye – because it creates a neat margin on the right-hand edge of the page – but it is generally harder to read and makes the spacing between words erratic. This paragraph is right-justified.

FONT STYLES

There are thousands of fonts, but they fall into two basic families:

- First are the *serif* fonts. This paragraph is in the serif font Times New Roman. Serifs are the small embellishments at the end of the characters: for example, the foot at the bottom of the letter T.
- Second are the *sans serif* fonts. This paragraph is in the sans serif font Arial. Sans serif fonts have no embellishments.

Sans serif fonts are usually considered easier to read. Many teachers like to use **Comic Sans** because of its reassuring, informal style. The main rule of fonts is not to combine too many in the same paragraph: it simply looks confusing.

OTHER LAYOUT FEATURES

A section of reversed text – white text on black shading – can add visual variety and draw the reader's attention to a new section of meaning. However, it can also give undue prominence to a minor subsection of information, and – depending on the font style and size – can prove difficult to read. Overused, it can become fussy and distracting.

Subheadings can help to guide a reader through the direction of a text's argument. Cross-headers are particularly useful: they pick out a key word from the paragraph that follows them, thus helping the reader to gain the gist of the text.

USING LAYOUT FEATURES TO MAKE TEXTS MORE ACCESSIBLE

Before asking pupils to read the texts, be clear why you are using them. Is it appropriate and accessible for all pupils?

 Aim for:

- Spacious presentation (as much white page as black text)
- Headlines and subheadings that capture the pupils' interest and lead them into a subject (for example, 'The shocking downfall: why does Macbeth sink from hero to villain?')
- Bold, italic, underline, different font styles and sizes (though not too many in a single document)
- Boxes, shaded panels, vertical lines to add visual interest
- Use of columns to make reading more efficient
- Short paragraphs
- Subheadings (especially cross-headers) to guide the reader
- Final summary of key facts/main information
- Glossary of key words

X Avoid:

- Densely packed writing
- Cramped margins
- Excessive use of upper-case lettering
- Poor reprographics
- Lack of images/typographical features
- Excessive use of colour (which can actually prove distracting)

HOW TO HELP PUPILS UNDERSTAND SUBJECT-SPECIFIC VOCABULARY

The DfES Secondary Strategy encourages us to view Key Stage 3 as securing the foundations for Key Stage 4. The more explicit teaching of subject-specific vocabulary should therefore take place at Key Stage 3.

In our language we use words from a range of registers or contexts. It can be helpful to think in terms of four registers:

Register	Definition
The common register	The most common, everyday words in our language. By some linguists' estimates there are around 500,000 of these.
The colloquial register	The informal words we use, including slang expressions. These words and expressions will vary according to audience and our background. They will often change rapidly over time.
The literary register	Words associated with literature.
The technical/scientific register	Words associated with science and technology.

The reason this is important is that it can highlight the way words change their meanings according to context. While pupils may be familiar with a word in its common register use, they may need explicit teaching about its meaning in other contexts. For example:

Word	Common register meaning	Technical meanings
Plates	Dishes used for eating	Geography: rigid slabs made of the Earth's crust that move relative to one another
Frequency	How often something happens	Physics: the rate at which an electrical current alternates
Highlight	Best part	Art: the lightest or whitest parts in a photograph or illustration represented in half-tone reproduction by the smallest dots or the absence of dots
Tone	The way something sounds	Linguistics: a pitch or change in pitch of the voice that serves to distinguish words in tonal languages Literature: the quality of a piece of writing that reveals the attitude of the author

This is an important reminder that we cannot take our pupils' recognition of subject-specific vocabulary for granted. We need to teach it.

HOW TO HELP PUPILS UNDERSTAND SUBJECT-SPECIFIC VOCABULARY

YOUR KNOWLEDGE

What is the essential subject-specific vocabulary that pupils need to know for your subject? Which words do we want all Year 7 pupils to know about language, literature and media? If you teach another subject, what are the key words there, again on a year-by-year basis?

Across the teaching team, is there agreement about the meanings of these words and that they need to be explicitly taught? (A good starting-point for discussion is the QCA spelling lists, issued a few years ago.) You're not going to be able to teach the vocabulary effectively if you haven't a clear view of what the essential words are.

To support pupils' vocabulary development:

- Display the key words in your classroom, with definitions.

- Post them on your department's intranet site.

- Draw attention to affixes that will help pupils to make connections with other words – for example:

    Auto + bio + graphy = self + life + writing

Can pupils think of other words containing any of these three elements? Do they share a similar meaning?

- Encourage pupils to have personal word books where they collect subject-specific vocabulary and definitions from all their subjects.

- Build glossaries into handouts. This will help pupils to know the meaning of specific words and develop their skills in using reference strategies like glossaries, contents lists and indexes.

To build these strategies into your lesson design:

- Plan a sequence of starters built around subject-specific vocabulary – for example, pupils in teams spotting the correct spelling/definition of literary terms like 'metaphor', 'simile', 'hyperbole'.

- Use plenary sessions to refer back to key words, asking pupils to think of good definitions for different audiences – for example, how would you explain metaphor to a six-year-old?

- Encourage pupils to work in small groups or pairs to discuss the meanings of words. Get them to brainstorm how a word such as 'image' or 'tone' might be used differently in other subjects.

- Tell pupils that you will be rewarding successful use of subject-specific vocabulary in their next essay – ask them to highlight the words, to which you might add a big tick or smiley face.

HOW TO TEACH DIFFERENT APPROACHES TO READING

It is worth remembering that we read for different purposes. This counts across texts as well as within texts. In other words, sometimes we will read a newspaper for pleasure; sometimes to get the gist of a story; sometimes to find out some specific information. The same applies to many other texts – recipe books, novels, autobiographies.

In schools we often don't give enough attention to this. We can easily assume that reading is all about comprehension.

There are four broad approaches to reading which you need to know about:

Approach	Definition
Scanning	Searching a text for a specific piece of information – for example, a quotation
Skimming	Glancing through a text to get the gist – for example, using subheadings and topic sentences to pick up a writer's general argument
Continuous reading	Uninterrupted reading of an extended text – for example, a novel
Close reading	Studying a text in detail, which involves moving back and forth through the text – for example, studying the presentation of a theme or character in a short story

When working with pupils, we should aim to make our expectations of the appropriate approach more explicit. This will help them to use the appropriate approach and to recognise their own growing ability to read in different ways for different purposes.

HOW TO TEACH DIFFERENT APPROACHES TO READING

BEFORE THE LESSON

Before using a text with pupils, be clear which approach to reading they will need. Are you expecting them to locate specific pieces of information, or to gain an overview of the text? Will they need to analyse it in detail? Is the intention for them to read for pleasure?

DURING THE LESSON

Teach pupils explicitly about the way we read for different purposes. Have the four reading approaches on display in your room, so that they can refer to them.

Use a sequence of starter activities to get pupils thinking about how they might approach the reading of a certain text – for example:

> **You have been given a textbook in geography and asked to list the five main facts explaining how volcanoes erupt. Which approach to reading will you use? How will you approach the task?**

> Next: **You are reading a novel set on a volcanic island. You have been asked to look at the way the writer builds suspense. Which approach to reading will you use?**

Talk to pupils about how you read – model the process. Talk about the book you are currently reading for pleasure. Explain how sometimes you might use the same book for a different reading purpose (for example, to find a quotation, to check some details, to study how the writer uses language).

Explicitly teach pupils how to scan a text. Use starter activities to give out a series of mystery texts (for example, pages from recipe books, openings of stories, historical writing, science writing, a leaflet, and so on). For each one, give pupils a short amount of time (for example, 90 seconds) with the task of either locating some specific information or gaining the overall gist of the text. After 90 seconds, pupils move round to the next text. Working like this in pairs or small groups will build pupils' awareness of different reading approaches and build their confidence. In the plenary, get them to talk about how they approach the task, how their skills are developing and what they are learning about how people read.

WHOLE SCHOOL

Encourage a whole school approach to adopting these approaches to reading. It will give further clarity and reassurance to pupils.

DEVELOPING PUPILS' RESEARCH SKILLS

Pupils are frequently expected to read a text and locate information. This happens in most subject areas across school. However, pupils are rarely taught how to approach such tasks, with the result that some struggle with the activity and lose confidence in their own reading abilities.

A systematic approach to research projects will pay dividends, both in the quality of the work pupils produce, their increased understanding of the process, and better motivation for similar projects.

This approach to research is from Wray and Lewis, who outline the following four-stage process:

Stage 1: Establishing purpose	This stage is about providing a context. It helps pupils to understand what they are being expected to find out, how this links with their existing knowledge, and being clear about the outcome that is expected
Stage 2: Locating information	This helps pupils to focus on the practicalities of the task – what sources of information to use, the reading approaches they might need and how to record their findings
Stage 3: Interacting with the text	This should be an active stage – finding information, making judgements about its relevance and value, finding appropriate ways of noting it
Stage 4: Shaping and communicating information	This is the outcome phase in which pupils think about how best to organise and present their findings. The better the original definition of the required outcome, the more likely pupils are to achieve it successfully

Throughout the research process the aim should be for pupils not simply to find out and present the required information. They should also be reflecting on their own developing reading skills – how they are approaching the task, the skills they are employing, how they are overcoming difficulties and, in short, what they are learning about their own learning.

DEVELOPING PUPILS' RESEARCH SKILLS

BEFORE THE LESSON

Be clear what the purpose of the task is. Too often in schools research projects can be formless and too long, keeping pupils busy for a fair amount of time but not necessarily developing their reading skills or understanding of a subject in a way that merits the amount of the time devoted to it.

STAGE 1: ESTABLISHING PURPOSE

- Spend time setting up the project: be really specific about the final outcome, both in terms of the form (a poster, a presentation, a report) and also the audience (another class, younger readers, sixth-form pupils).

- Encourage pupils to link the project to their prior learning: what they already know about the topic. Give them a short time to explore their existing learning and to ask some questions of their own about what they want to find out.

STAGE 2: LOCATING INFORMATION

- Link this stage to approaches to reading: get pupils thinking about which approaches they will use. Remember – the focus should be on the 'how' of the task (the process) as much as the 'what' (the final product).

- Focus pupils on the range of possible information sources. Use some skills-building activities to remind them how to use contents pages and indexes. Have part of a lesson in the library, with a ten-minute reminder from the librarian about information retrieval skills. Devise a mini-lesson which teaches pupils about using the internet. Set a topic such as a famous author. Get them to road-test different search engines and compare the results.

STAGE 3: INTERACTING WITH THE TEXT

- Get pupils to think about the best way of recording information – for example, road-test different grids and tables.

- Use starters to teach note-taking. Give a mini-lecture and ask pupils to make notes in different ways – using subheadings, using a spider diagram, using a table, using diagrams, using no structure at all. Get them talking about how they approached the task and how well they feel they did. Get them to decide, for their individual learning style, which approach suits them best.

- Explore the difference between fact and opinion – for example, use a newspaper story versus editorial; look at extracts from an authorised/unauthorised biography.

STAGE 4: SHAPING AND COMMUNICATING INFORMATION

- Get pupils talking about how to take their research and re-present it in the required format.

- Spend some time focusing on the ingredients of an effective poster/PowerPoint/report. Look at text-type conventions. Compare good/bad models – for example, demonstrating the tedium of endless bullet points and sound effects in PowerPoint presentations. Consider who the audience is.

- Draw the project together by focusing not only on the quality of the finished products but also on the process – for example: How has your research work improved? What reading skills have you developed? What have you learnt?

THEORY

USING DIRECTED ACTIVITIES RELATED TO TEXTS

Traditional school comprehension was often remorselessly tedious. Pupils would read a text and then face a seemingly endless set of questions, many of which tested nothing other than a narrow ability to spot key words or facts.

Here's an example of how artificial that process can be. This is a nonsense text and yet you will be able to answer the questions – namely, without understanding what the text is about.

TRUSLERS

Most truslers were fungicated in Whippyville. They were frequently stoggled into pashwit bloatings, foibled, and disconvetoed within snoozlings, traceys or snargets. Their thumpwacking sistings were also transcretined into chevin.

1   Where were most truslers fungicated?

2   What were they were stoggled into?

3   Name one thing they were disconvetoed within.

Directed activities related to texts (DARTs) are more active ways of getting pupils to process and respond to texts. Pupils like them because they resemble games and puzzles. They work well as pair or group activities. They encourage an exploratory approach, rather than a simple right/wrong answer.

DARTs fall in two main categories:

Reconstruction activities

- Text completion (cloze)
- Diagram completion
- Table completion
- Completion activities with disordered text
- Prediction

Analysis activities

- Underlining or highlighting
- Labelling
- Segmenting
- Diagrammatic representation
- Tabular representation

DARTs help us to get away from an over reliance on questions, whether in writing or live in class. But you need to prepare them, and your starting point should be 'What do I want pupils to learn from this text?' That emphasis on learning is important because, however entertaining the DARTs approach can be, it can also be unproductive if not clearly focused on developing specific reading skills.

USING DIRECTED ACTIVITIES RELATED TO TEXTS

ACTIVITIES FOR RECONSTRUCTING TEXTS

Text completion (cloze)	Give pupils a text in which certain key words, phrases and sentences have been deleted. Working in pairs or small groups, pupils work out what the omissions are. Train them to tell you why they made certain predictions – what the language clues were.
Diagram completion	Ask pupils to predict what the missing labels on a diagram might be, based on their reading of a text and other diagrams – for example, an explanation text.
Table completion	Give pupils a text to read and a table with deliberate gaps and omissions. Based on their reading, they predict what the gaps might be – for example, studying different characters in a novel.
Disordered text	Give pupils a text in the wrong sequence, perhaps cut up on to strips of paper. Pupils predict the correct sequence – for example, by focusing on connectives ('such as', 'firstly}, 'next') and pronouns ('he', 'they'). Remember always to ask pupils in their feedback to describe the basis for their decisions – namely, the process they went through.
Prediction	Withhold the next part of the text, either by not handing it out, or simply by asking pupils to look up and turn the text over. What do they think happens next? What clues are there? Give them thinking time, and time to consult with a partner, before requiring an answer.

ACTIVITIES FOR ANALYSING TEXTS

Underlining or highlighting	Ask pupils to find examples of something and mark them directly on to the text – for example, an image, emotive words, certain types of sentences.
Labelling	Ask pupils to annotate a text – for example, labelling a passage to show what we learn about a character.
Segmenting	Ask pupils to break a text into paragraphs or sections and explain – for example, showing how an author has structured a text with sections of plot, dialogue and description.
Diagrammatic representation	Ask pupils to convert a text into a diagram or graph – for example, using a graph to show how a writer builds suspense in different paragraphs.
Tabular representation	Ask pupils to find certain pieces of information and then to present it in a table or grid, which they devise.

Remember – all of these can be entertaining activities in their own right. Keep focusing on the learning, asking pupils to demonstrate what they have learnt about their own reading skills from the process.

THEORY

TEACHING PUPILS TO MAKE NOTES

Pupils are frequently asked, across all their subjects, to make notes. Too often they will be given a textbook or handout and blithely given the task of making notes. Some pupils will copy out chunks; others will write down lists of facts or information, irrespective of their relevance; others will do the task supremely well.

Few teachers, it seems, teach pupils how to make notes consistently and effectively.

Key Stage 3 is when we should be ensuring that our pupils can make notes well, that they know what the phrase means and can do such tasks confidently and successfully, ready for Key Stage 4 and beyond.

Making notes involves a complex set of skills, including:

- Close reading, listening, watching
- Making sense of an original text
- Determining what is relevant
- Identifying relationships between ideas
- Understanding how the writer has arrived at the key ideas
- Critically reflecting on the validity of the ideas in the text
- Selecting ideas appropriate to the task
- Transforming the language of the original into a form which is meaningful to the reader, even when they are producing an aide-mémoire for themselves
- Abbreviating language to produce a summary

(*Developing Reading: Pedagogy and Practice: Teaching and Learning in Secondary Schools*, DfES)

Pupils will really benefit from a cross-curricular approach to note-making, so that all teachers share the same conventions and expectations.

PRACTICE

TEACHING PUPILS TO MAKE NOTES

BEFORE THE LESSON

If you are asking pupils to make notes, think about why they have to do it. What purpose will their notes serve? How detailed do they need to be? What do you envisage as a good set of notes? How detailed? How long? In what format? If you aren't clear about your expectations, and you don't communicate them, then don't be surprised if pupils' note-making skills prove inconsistent.

DURING THE LESSON

Focus on the micro-skills of note-making, as listed on the opposite page. If you want pupils to make notes as they watch a video, then model the process. Using a sample video extract, show them:

- How to manage the task (for example, articulating the purpose of the task, using subheadings to note key information, using abbreviations to get information down quickly)
- What your own notes might look like
- How you decided what was and wasn't relevant

Then let pupils practise, working in pairs to make notes on a different sequence. Get pairs of pupils comparing their notes with others' so that learning about note-making becomes a collaborative venture.

Use starter activities to practise note-making. Give pupils a sequence of two-minute mini-lectures on different topics for each starter (for example, my memories of childhood; how to edit a film) and require them to listen and make notes. Talk about the skills involved and the format of the notes. Get them comparing the finished results.

Use plenary sessions to get pupils articulating their developing confidence in note-making. What are the three most important skills? How do they decide what to note down and what to ignore? What have they learnt about note-making that they didn't know at the start of the lesson/week/term?

Link note-making to relevant grammatical principles – in particular, topic sentences and connectives. Demonstrate to pupils how writers use these to help the reader to follow ideas.

SUMMARY

The key messages of this section are:

- Teaching reading is part of every teacher's responsibility.

- English teachers have shared responsibility for the vocabulary pupils need in other subjects – make as many connections as possible and break down the compartmentalisation of the curriculum.

- All teachers need to have a systematic approach to teaching reading.

- We need to make explicit many of the processes and strategies we use when reading.

- We need to be clear about purpose and audience.

- Attention to language and layout can make even demanding subject matter much more accessible.

The challenges include:

- What scaffolding will your *least confident readers* need (for example, glossaries, summaries, simpler versions of a text, being paired with a more confident reader, being given sufficient time to read, being given strategies for getting through a long or demanding text)?

- What will you give to your *most accomplished readers* to challenge them (for example, extracts from other, more demanding texts (such as original science or history texts); tasks that move them beyond mere comprehension to synthesising and evaluating ideas in a text and then presenting and justifying their response?

Glossary

Ablaut	The process of inflecting a verb by changing its vowel: s<u>i</u>ng, s<u>a</u>ng, s<u>u</u>ng.

Active and passive
(See p. 18)

The passive voice turns a sentence around so that the object comes first and the subject is placed later – like this:

The wind destroyed the greenhouse (*active*).

The passive voice places emphasis on what happened rather than who did it:

The greenhouse was destroyed by the wind (*passive*).

The passive voice will sometimes leave the subject out altogether:

The greenhouse was destroyed (*passive*).

The passive voice is not very common in most speech and writing. It is, however, a feature of certain text types: scientific, technical and legal writing, as well as some journalism, which sometimes adopts the passive voice.
It can be useful where the speaker/writer wishes to:
- Withhold information
- Conceal information
- Build suspense
- Give emphasis to what happened rather than who did it

Adjective
(See pp. 9, 16)

A word that describes or qualifies a noun or pronoun – e.g.
It was a <u>tedious</u> match.

She is <u>vile</u>.

Adjectives add descriptive power by qualifying a noun (We made a <u>late</u> start) or reinforcing it (He possessed a <u>hypnotic</u> charm).

Adverb
(See p.9)

A word which gives more information about a verb, adjective or other adverb. Adverbs can tell us about:
- Manner (he walked <u>slowly</u>)
- Place (he walked <u>there</u>)
- Time (he walked <u>yesterday</u>)
- Gradation (we don't see him <u>enough</u>)
- Frequency (we <u>hardly ever</u> go there)
- Viewpoint (I wouldn't travel, <u>personally</u>)
- A link to an earlier idea (<u>therefore</u> he left)
- Attitude (<u>strangely</u>, it vanished)

The idea that adverbs usually end '-ly' isn't always helpful: <u>quite, very, so</u> are all adverbs. Nor is it helpful to think that adverbs only modify verbs:

He moved <u>wearily</u> down the winding lane (*modifying a verb*).

He moved wearily down the <u>gently</u> winding lane (*modifying an adjective*).

He moved <u>very wearily</u> down the <u>gently</u> winding lane (*modifying an adverb*).

It is useful to encourage pupils to avoid piling adverbs up in their writing.

Agreement
(See p.49)

The process in which a verb is altered to match the number, person and gender of its subject or object: 'he smiles' (not 'smile') versus 'they smile' (not 'smiles'). This is an important issue when comparing Standard English with other dialects, as agreement is often one point of difference.

Apostrophe
(See p.38)

A punctuation mark, used to clarify two types of meaning.
1 It shows when some letters have been omitted ('is' + 'not' = 'isn't'). We use this type of expression more in informal situations.
2 It shows that something belongs to someone ('Pete's holiday'). The apostrophe can inform the reader about whether the noun is singular (just one) or plural (more than one) according to its position. For example: in 'We saw the vandal's damage' the

GLOSSARY

placing of the apostrophe after *vandal* shows that there is just one vandal. In *We saw the vandals' damage* the apostrophe is placed after the plural, <u>vandals</u>, so that there is more than one vandal.

Note the use of apostrophes for possession in: <u>in a week's time</u> and <u>in two years' time</u>. Note that <u>its</u> is a pronoun, like *her* and *his*, and has a different meaning from <u>it's</u> (= <u>it is</u>)

Article

A word class containing words that modify a noun, such as <u>the</u>, <u>a</u>, <u>an</u> and <u>some</u>. Nowadays usually subsumed in the determiner category.

Auxiliary verb
(See p.2)

This is a verb form we put in front of a main verb to change its meaning. There are two main types:
1   Primary auxiliaries: <u>be</u>, <u>do</u>, <u>have</u> (e.g. I <u>am</u> speaking; you <u>do</u> speak; you <u>have</u> spoken).
2   Modal auxiliaries: <u>can</u>/<u>could</u>, <u>may</u>/<u>might</u> <u>must</u>, <u>shall</u>/<u>should</u>, <u>will</u>/<u>would</u>. Auxiliaries allow us to express a huge range of meanings and emotions (especially if we add <u>not</u>):
  • I <u>have</u> not spoken.
  • I <u>would</u> speak.
  • I <u>could</u> have spoken.
  • I <u>would</u> not have been speaking.

Back-formation

The process of creating a simple word from a complex word not originally derived from the simple word – e.g. 'to burgle' (from 'burglar').

Bahuvrihi

A compound word that refers to someone by what he or she does rather than what he or she is – e.g. 'four-eyes', 'cut-throat'.

Clause
(See p.36)

A group of words formed around a verb. They are used to make up sentences. This compound sentence contains two clauses linked by 'and':
The complex sentence below also contains two clauses. One is the **main clause** (it carries the main information). The second is the **subordinate** or **dependent clause** (it gives background detail):
The car left the track, leaving the crowd terrified.

Collocation

String of words commonly used together, 'in the line of fire'.

Colon
(See p.36)

Punctuation mark which shows that something else follows within the sentence. Useful to precede lists and quotations, but also building anticipation: 'She knew as she opened the door that there was danger: she was right.'

Comma
(See p.30)

Commas are used:
  • To separate items in a list or strings of adjectives, e.g. 'the dark, mysterious substance'.
  • To introduce direct speech and replace the full stop at the end of the spoken sentence ('He said, "Hi." "Hello," she replied.').
  • To mark off a relative clause, e.g. 'The light, which had seemed so strong, had now faded.'
  • To mark off many connecting adverbs, e.g. 'Ruthlessly, he lifted the sword.'
  • To attach a question tag to a statement, e.g. 'This makes sense, doesn't it?'
  • After a subordinate clause or phrase which begins a sentence, e.g. 'Despite the terrible snow, he set off home.'

Parenthetical commas, in pairs, bracket off a word, phrase or clause: 'The house, abandoned eight years ago, had lights on.'

Compound

Word formed by joining two words together – e.g. 'babysitter', 'blackbird'.

Conjunction
(See pp.10, 44)

A word used for joining words, phrases and clauses within sentences. The most commonly-used examples are 'and', 'but', 'or'.

Connective
(See p.44)

A word or phrase that helps us to make connections between different ideas in a text. Typical examples include: 'on the other hand', 'however', 'in fact'. Each of these hints that the sentence or paragraph which follows will connect with what has gone before – giving a different argument ('on the other hand'/'however') or adding more information ('in fact').

Conversion

Deriving a new word by changing the word class of the old word – e.g. 'to impact' (from noun 'impact'), 'a good read' (from verb 'to read').

Dashes

Punctuation marks used to add information, or – sometimes – to bracket off ideas.

Determiner (See p.16)	Word class containing articles and similar words before nouns and noun phrases: eg 'a', 'the', 'their', 'more', 'many', 'my'.
Dialect (See p.48)	A variety of English. Standard English, although a minority dialect, is prestigious because it is used in education, law, the media, and is the dialect used for most written forms.
Diphthong	Vowel sound consisting of two vowels pronounced together (eg b*i*te, m*a*ke).
Direct speech (See p.32)	A speaker's words or thoughts, placed within speech marks.
Dynamic and stative verbs	Dynamic verbs describe actions ('to hit', 'to travel', 'to jump'). Stative verbs describe states of mind ('to think', 'to hope', 'to be').
Early modern English	The English of Shakespeare and King James Bible, spoken and written from around 1450 to 1700.
Eponym	Noun derived from a name – e.g. 'a scrooge', 'a hoover', a 'boycott'.
Exclamation mark	Punctuation mark used to show urgency or emotion!
Full stop (See p.28)	Punctuation mark used to mark the ends of sentences.
Gerund	Noun formed out of a verb by adding -ing (e.g. 'his constant <u>whining</u>').
Head (See p.16)	The key word in a phrase that determines the meaning of the whole – e.g. 'the <u>man</u> in the grey suit', 'the old grey <u>lizard</u>'.
Homophones	Words that are identical in sound ('their'/'there'; 'no'/'know').
Hyphen	Punctuation mark used to join two words together ('second-hand' means something different from 'second hand').
Imperative	Form of a verb used to give a command – e.g. 'jump!'
Infinitive	Form of a verb that lacks a tense and stands for the verb as a whole – e.g. 'to think'.
Inflection	The way words change their shape to show, for example, that they are singular or plural (e.g. 'door' becomes 'doors') and to indicate tense (eg 'think' becomes 'thinks'/'thought').
Intransitive	Verb that can appear without an object – e.g. 'We dined' (as opposed to 'He devoured the steak' – 'devoured' cannot stand without the object).
Irregular form	Word with an unusual inflected form rather than following the usual rules of inflection (e.g. 'brought' not 'bringed', 'mice' not 'mouses').
Middle English	Language spoken and written in England shortly after the Norman invasion in 1066 to the Great Vowel Shift of the 1400s.
Minor sentence (See p.2)	A sentence which contains no verb. Advertising uses a lot of minor sentences: 'Ahh Bisto!' 'The ultimate driving machine'. Sometimes they might be answers to questions: 'Yes'. Exclamations are also frequently presented as minor sentences: 'Agghh!'
Modern English	Variety of English spoken and written since the eighteenth century.
Modification (See p.44)	Modification allows us to add detail to texts. For example, we can . . . : • Modify a noun with an adjective: 'the <u>old</u> taxi'. • Modify a noun with a phrase: 'the taxi <u>in the street</u>'. • Modify a noun with a clause: 'the taxi <u>which smelt awful</u>'. • Modify an adjective with an adverb: 'the <u>very</u> old taxi'. • Modify a verb with an adverb: 'the taxi was waiting <u>noisily</u>'. • Modify a verb with a phrase: 'the taxi was waiting <u>in the street</u>'. • Modify a verb with a clause: 'the taxi was waiting, <u>which made me worried</u>'.
Morpheme	A group of letters which cannot stand on their own, but they can be added to root words to change their meaning (e.g. 'pre-', 'de-', '-ly').
Noun (See p.16)	A word which labels a person, thing or idea. There are four types of noun: • Common: the 'radio', a 'cloud'

- Proper: 'Mike', 'Woolworth'
- Abstract: 'peace', 'hope'
- Collective: 'herd' of goats, 'pod' of whales

Old English Language spoken and written in England from around 450 to 1100.

Paragraph A group of sentences linked together by their theme or topic. Paragraphs are useful in
(See p.42) fiction in texts for a number of effects:
- Change of speaker
- Change of time
- Change of place
- Change of viewpoint

In non-fiction texts, paragraphs are used for these reasons:

- Change of topic.
- To make new point within topic
- Change of time
- Change of viewpoint

Participle Form of the verb which cannot stand alone but needs an auxiliary or other verb in front –
e.g. 'He has <u>eaten</u>' (perfect participle)', 'He was <u>eaten</u>' (passive participle), 'He is <u>eating</u>'
(present participle).

Passive voice See Active and passive.
(See p.18)

Phrase A group of words which makes sense within a clause or sentence but cannot stand on its
(See p.3) own – e.g. 'the unpleasant smell', 'shouting loudly'.

Pluperfect A past tense showing an action that has already been completed some time ago in the past:
'When I arrived, John <u>had fainted</u>.'

Plural More than one. Most nouns add +'s' to make a plural. Some nouns are only plural:
'scissors', 'jeans' (called pluralia tantum, in case you're interested). Some are singular and
plural: 'sheep'.

Prefix Letters added to the beginning of a word to change its meaning (e.g. <u>dis</u> + 'honour').

Preposition A word used chiefly to show where something or someone is: 'under', 'through', 'on'.

Preterite Simple past-tense form of a verb – e.g. 'he walked', 'he sang' (as opposed to using participle
'he has walked').

Progressive Verb form that shows an ongoing event – e.g. 'He is <u>waving</u> his hands.'

Pronoun A word which can be used in place of a noun – e.g. 'The Prime Minister visited today. Did
(See p.44) <u>you</u> see <u>him</u>?'

Punctuation The marks we use in writing to help the reader understand our ideas. Their use can be vital
(See p.27) in clarifying our meaning, as in this classic example: 'King Charles I prayed half an hour
after he was beheaded' (a strategically placed full stop changes the meaning).

Question mark Punctuation mark used to indicate that the sentence is a question. In speech, we raise the
pitch of our voice at the end to show that the sentence is a question.

Register The way we change our use of language in different situations. We might use a formal
(See p.52) register in an interview ('I am particularly interested in socialising with friends') or an
informal register with friends ('Fancy a drink?').

Relative clauses A group of words built around a verb that you can add to sentences to give more detail.
(See p.14) Take a simple sentence like 'My bedroom is a bombsite.' Add a relative clause after the
subject: 'My bedroom, which I tidied last week, is a bombsite.'

You can add relative clauses at other points too:

'My bedroom is a bombsite, which is very annoying'.

Relative pronouns Words such as 'who', 'which' and 'that' used at the start of relative clauses.

Root words Words which we can add prefixes and suffixes to in order to change their meanings.

Schwa The neutral vowels in 'moth<u>er</u>',' accid<u>e</u>nt', 'stat<u>io</u>n'.

Semi-colon
(See p.34)

Punctuation mark somewhere in strength between a full stop and a comma. It often replaces the word 'and' between clauses and phrases.

Sentence
(See p.2)

A group of words which can stand on their own. We expect sentences to:

- Contain a main verb
- Begin with a capital letter
- End with a full stop, question mark or exclamation mark

Sentence functions

The purposes of sentences: statements, questions, commands and exclamations.

Sentence types
(See pp.2–13)

Simple, compound and complex.

Singular

See Plural.

Standard English
(See p.48)

The most important dialect or variety of English. It is used in most written texts, in education, in law, in the media. It is the form of English defined in dictionaries.

Stem

The main portion of a word that prefixes and suffixes are added to.

Subject and object
(See p.18)

The subject is the person or thing in a sentence that is doing the action of the verb. (In 'Helen threw the towel to Lucy' 'Helen' is the subject – she is doing the throwing).

Subjunctive

Verb form that indicates a hypothetical state of affairs – e.g. 'If I <u>were</u> you'.

Suffix

Letters added to the end of a word to change its meaning – e.g. peace+<u>ful</u>.

Synonym

A word which has a similar meaning to another word. Synonyms for 'house' include: 'home', 'abode', 'my place', 'pad'. You would choose different words according to the register you used.

Tense
(See p.20)

English changes the ending of verbs to show the present and past tenses:

She laugh + s ... she laugh + <u>ed</u>.

To show the future tense, we sometimes use the present tense verb with an adverbial:

The bus leaves <u>later</u>.

The bus leaves <u>in three minutes</u>.

The bus leaves <u>next week</u>.

We can also create the future tense by using modal verbs – 'will'/'would'/'shall'/'might'.

The bus <u>will</u> leave in three minutes.

The bus <u>might</u> leave next week.

Topic sentence
(See p.42)

A sentence at the start of a text or paragraph which tells you what the content will be. Newspaper stories usually start with topic sentences: they tell you who, where, when. Example:

Local headteacher Howard Lay, 44, was recovering from a bizarre accident at school last night.

Verb
(See p.2)

A word which tells us what someone or something is doing – e.g.

She <u>noticed</u> the car. It <u>came</u> to a halt.

Verb phrase
(See p.2)

Sometimes we use a number of verbs together to add detail, for example about tense (when something happened). For example:

I see

see = main verb

I have seen = verb phrase (seen = main verb, have = auxiliary verb)

I will see = verb phrase (see = main verb, will = auxiliary verb)

I would have seen = verb phrase (seen = main verb, would = auxiliary verb, have = auxiliary verb)

Word class

A group of words with a particular function in a sentence – nouns, verbs, adjectives, adverbs, prepositions, conjunctions, and so on.

Further Reading

ENGLISH TEACHING

Clarke, S., Dickinson, P., Westbrook, J. (2004) *The Complete Guide to Becoming an English Teacher*. Paul Chapman Publishing, London.

Davison, J. and Dowson, J. (1998) *Learning to Teach English in the Secondary School: A Companion to School Experience*. Routledge, London.

Dean, G. (2004) *Improving Learning in Secondary English*. David Fulton, London.

DfES (2004) *Developing Reading: Pedagogy and Practice: Teaching and Learning in Secondary Schools*. London: DfES.

GRAMMAR

Barton, G. (1999) *Grammar in Context*. Oxford University Press, Oxford.

Barton, G. (2001) *Active Grammar*. Oxford University Press, Oxford.

Crystal, D. (1995) *The Cambridge Encyclopedia of the English Language*. Cambridge University Press, Cambridge.

Crystal, D. (1998) *Rediscover Grammar*. Longman, Harlow.

McArthur, T. (ed), (1992) *The Oxford Companion to the English Language*. Oxford University Press, Oxford.

Thomas, H. (1999) *Grammar and Punctuation*. Scholastic, London.

Thorne, S. *Mastering Advanced English Language*. Macmillan, Basingstoke.

Trask, R.L. (1995) *Language: The Basics*. Routledge, London.

Truss, L. (2003) *Eats, Shoots and Leaves*. Profile Books, London.